teach yourself

jung

teach yourself ®

jung
ruth snowden

For over 60 years, more than
40 million people have learnt over
750 subjects the **teach yourself**
way, with impressive results.

be where you want to be
with **teach yourself**

With thanks to Richard Chapman, the illustrator of this book.

For UK order enquiries: please contact Bookpoint Ltd, 130 Milton Park, Abingdon, Oxon OX14 4SB. Telephone: +44 (0) 1235 827720. Fax: +44 (0) 1235 400454. Lines are open 09.00–18.00, Monday to Saturday, with a 24-hour message answering service. Details about our titles and how to order are available at www.teachyourself.co.uk

For USA order enquiries: please contact McGraw-Hill Customer Services, PO Box 545, Blacklick, OH 43004-0545, USA. Telephone: 1-800-722-4726. Fax: 1-614-755-5645.

For Canada order enquiries: please contact McGraw-Hill Ryerson Ltd, 300 Water St, Whitby, Ontario L1N 9B6, Canada. Telephone: 905 430 5000. Fax: 905 430 5020.

Long renowned as the authoritative source for self-guided learning – with more than 40 million copies sold worldwide – the **teach yourself** series includes over 300 titles in the fields of languages, crafts, hobbies, business, computing and education.

British Library Cataloguing in Publication Data: a catalogue record for this title is available from the British Library.

Library of Congress Catalog Card Number: on file.

First published in UK 2006 by Hodder Education, 338 Euston Road, London, NW1 3BH.

First published in US 2006 by Contemporary Books, a Division of the McGraw-Hill Companies, 1 Prudential Plaza, 130 East Randolph Street, Chicago, IL 60601 USA.

This edition published 2006.

The **teach yourself** name is a registered trade mark of Hodder Headline.

Typeset by Transet Limited, Coventry, England.
Printed in Great Britain for Hodder Education, a division of Hodder Headline, 338 Euston Road, London NW1 3BH, by Cox & Wyman Ltd, Reading, Berkshire.

Hodder Headline's policy is to use papers that are natural, renewable and recyclable products and made from wood grown in sustainable forests. The logging and manufacturing processes are expected to conform to the environmental regulations of the country of origin.

Impression number   10 9 8 7 6 5 4 3 2 1
Year   2010 2009 2008 2007 2006

contents

Carl Jung (1875–1961) was a Swiss **psychologist** and **psychiatrist** who is famous for founding a new system of psychology that he called 'analytical psychology'. Jung has gradually acquired a huge following and many therapists today are trained in the Jungian method. However, his work also contains many important insights into the lives of humankind, far beyond the field of therapy, that have only recently begun to be more widely understood. He was one of the first great thinkers to try and bridge gaps between the thinking of East and West, Christian and pagan. He demonstrated ways in which Western culture, so bound up in science and logic, was often sadly deficient in the **spiritual** awareness and subjective insight shown in other cultures and at other times in history.

Jung is now a well-known figure worldwide and many books have been written about him and his work. Some of his ideas and the terms that he coined have found their way into everyday use today, for example the words **archetype** and 'introvert'. He was a prolific writer – his work stretches to over 20 volumes – and much of what we know about Jung's life and work can be found in his autobiography, *Memories, Dreams, Reflections,* which was recorded and edited by his friend and long-term assistant Aniela Jaffé. The short quotes from Jung in this book have been taken from a translation of this title (see **Further reading** on page 155), unless otherwise stated.

Jung was born towards the end of the nineteenth century, at a time when great changes were taking place in society, particularly in the field of science. Charles Darwin's (1809–82) theory of evolution had challenged religious thinking, causing people to question the truth of what was written in the Bible. Sigmund Freud (1856–1939) was expanding people's awareness of the importance of the **unconscious** in human psychology. Even the structure of society was changing, and people were searching for new truths and becoming more interested in self-knowledge.

Jung was a great scholar and his interests were wide ranging, covering such areas as astrology, **alchemy**, Gnosticism, archaeology and world religions, as well as psychology, psychiatry and medicine, in which he had originally trained. He was adept at languages – he mastered Latin, Greek, French and English in addition to his native German. His thinking and his work sprang not only from these interests, but also from his practical experience working with people who came to see him professionally.

Jung's research covered many spiritual traditions, because he was trying to search for truths that were common to all mankind. Frequently, he turned to the mystical and spiritual teachings of the East, as well as looking at Western traditions. This was not done as a rejection of his own culture, but rather in order to seek wholeness, and fill in the gaps he saw in both ways of thinking. As a result, his writing is of interest to people from both Eastern and Western cultures, helping them to understand one another better.

Jung found many symbols in Eastern philosophy and religion that reflected his own dreams and visions, often in startling ways. He became fascinated by the way these common themes ran through the myths and cultures of so many different people. For him they reflected the underlying inner knowlede, like a vast invisible sea, that he believed linked all human thinking. This led him to the idea of the **collective unconscious**, which is one of the central themes in Jungian teaching. The idea evolved partly from discussions with Freud, who was a friend and mentor to Jung and had a huge influence on him early in his career, until irreconcilable differences in their thinking eventually drove them apart. Freud had suggested that the developmental process in a child also reflected the entire history of the human race. Each individual has their own private life history, which emerges during dream work and analysis, but there is also a bigger picture, common to all of us, which manifests itself as built-in symbolic connections that the individual has not acquired by learning. Jung took Freud's idea a lot further and gave this deepest layer of the unconscious its name.

For Jung, a person's spiritual life was of paramount importance in the healing process. An individual's personal history was what mattered – Jung listened carefully to what his patients had to say on this subject. He regarded clinical diagnoses as being useful only to the doctor, for the purpose of giving him a frame of reference. He did not regard them as being helpful to the patient.

The emphasis on the importance of the individual, coupled with the underlying collective unconscious, meant that the system of analytical psychology that Jung developed was very much a spiritual psychology. This set it apart from the mainstream, which tended to be rigidly **mechanistic** in outlook. The mechanistic approach meant that doctors and scientists tended to see people as machines, whose behaviour was strictly determined by physical or chemical processes. Jung did not conform to this way of thinking: he had a lifelong fascination with the spiritual and the **numinous** (experiences that are awe-inspiring and uplifting, suggesting that there is a divine force at work in the universe). Jung said that such experiences formed the most important aspect of his work.

Jung coined the phrase 'analytical psychology' around 1913 in order to describe his work and to distinguish it from the system of **psychoanalysis**, originally developed by Freud. Analytical psychology is a whole system of psychology, which Jung developed gradually throughout his life. His ideas came from various sources:

- from nearly 60 years experience as a practising psychiatrist, studying the experiences of his patients
- through painstaking study of his own inner world and its dreams, visions and symbols
- by reading widely and travelling in order to explore the **myths** and religious beliefs of many cultures.

The main aspects of analytical psychology are that it:

- is a method of therapy, aimed not only at treating mental and nervous disorders, but also at helping ordinary people to become more balanced and self-aware
- attempts to provide a map of the human **psyche** in order to understand more fully how it works
- explores the deeper aspects of human psychology through the study of religious beliefs, dreams, myths, symbols and the **paranormal**.

Although Jung was extremely intelligent, he was always willing to learn from his patients, the majority of whom were women, and he found the dreams and images with which they presented him endlessly fascinating. He said that they constantly gave him insights into his own nature. He was a deeply spiritual person, and he was the first modern psychiatrist to recognize that the human psyche is 'religious' by nature, meaning that it is natural for us to seek that which is above and beyond our own sphere of existence. He referred to himself as a 'healer of the soul', exploring deep within his own psyche and those of his patients.

Jung based his psychology on explorations of his own inner world, as well his as work with people ranging from 'normal' to those with neurotic problems and even those who were suffering from **psychosis** (more extreme forms of mental illness). Jung was one of the first psychiatrists to attempt psychoanalysis with patients suffering from psychosis. Freud, the 'father of psychoanalysis', had warned against this, saying that such people were not suitable for analysis.

Freud and his followers were mainly concerned with early childhood trauma and the ways in which this affected a person's adult psyche. This meant that they focused mainly on the patient's past, stating that the first five years of life were all-important. Jung recognized that this was partly true, but he was more concerned with adult psychology, working with people who had largely moved on from this stage and were willing to take the personal development process further.

Many of Jung's patients seemed to him to be stuck because their thinking was too one-sided. He was very interested in the idea that the personality contains opposite and conflicting aspects – finding a balance between these was very important for individual progress. Jung said that it was essential for a person to understand their own psyche, and work with it in this way to achieve a sense of individuality, before they can achieve satisfactory relationships with others.

Jung always encouraged people to experience things for themselves and, where possible, to develop their own insights. So important was the inner world of the psyche to Jung that he regarded what he called the process of **individuation** as the central concept of his psychology. By this he means the lifelong journey that each of us must take in our gradual quest to become whole – a process of the conscious realization and fulfilment of the self. One of Jung's great strengths was his willingness to work on himself, and he never asked people to explore areas that he had not explored in his own psyche. He knew he had failings and was prepared to acknowledge them – he could be irritable, bad tempered and very demanding. When he was nearly 60, he said that his whole life had been a struggle to overcome childish traits, of which, regrettably, many still remained!

One of the techniques that Jung developed for exploring the psyche was what he called 'active imagination'. This was a process that he used both with his own inner exploration and with his patients'. It is a process a bit like a waking dreaming, where the patient is encouraged to enter a day-dream state and see where their fantasies lead. Jung then encouraged people to work further with their fantasies, for example by painting or drawing. He was the first analyst to extend verbal interaction with patients in this way – nowadays a whole host of therapies exist which are based on this method, such as art therapy and writing therapy.

It is now widely recognized that the unconscious mind affects the way people think and behave, as well as their general health and well-being. Throughout his work, Jung stressed the importance of the unconscious, as Freud had done. In Jung's day this idea was still relatively new – Freud was a pioneer in putting it forward as a scientific theory. But where Freud had seen the unconscious as a shadowy dumping ground for all that is primitive, childish and animal, such as repressed sexual urges, Jung saw it in a far more positive and expansive way. For him, it was a fascinating area to study and a rich source of creativity. Sadly, even today it is still common to dismiss ideas that spring from intuition and imagination. Jung saw this attitude as extremely limiting, calling it a 'nothing-but' attitude, because people tend to say that something is 'nothing but imagination', or 'just a coincidence'. Jung was fascinated by coincidences, dreams and intuitions – he paid close attention to them and learned from them all his life. For him, the inner world of the psyche with its dreams and visions was just as important as the outer world. Many people found his ideas hard to understand and saw him as a highly eccentric, even dangerous thinker.

Jung tended to use the word 'psyche', meaning the mind, soul or spirit – a term which covered both conscious and unconscious processes. 'Mind', on the other hand, was often used to imply concern only with conscious processes. Jung insists that the psyche is *real* – no less so than the physical world. He points out that everything that we are aware of is perceived and interpreted by the brain, so that in this sense all that we experience is actually 'psychic' in nature, and we can never actually know for certain the truth about the outside world. We can only make assumptions about the world based on our sensory impressions, and this means that each of us has our own unique way of looking at the world. We are so swamped all the time with the constant flow of sensory impressions that we cannot possibly have much idea of the true essence of things that exist outside ourselves. In effect, the psyche is the only reality. This is one of the main reasons that Jung emphasized the importance of inner exploration.

Towards the end of his life, Jung finally agreed to make an attempt to put some of his main ideas together in a way that was more understandable to ordinary people. The result was a book called *Man and his Symbols*, which makes a good starting point for studying Jung's ideas. The book emphasizes Jung's lifelong conviction that the inner world of the human psyche is of paramount importance and needs to be studied seriously.

Jung pointed out that analytical psychology can never be totally objective since the individual psyche always affects that which it is observing. Many people have criticized Jung for taking this stance, but perhaps he was just too far ahead of his time: advances in quantum physics have led scientists towards a startlingly similar conclusion (see Chapter 08). Recently there has been a big upsurge of interests in Jung's ideas, as people are becoming more willing to accept the idea that there is no clear division between the inner world of the psyche and the outer world of 'reality'.

Since Jung's death in 1961, his analysis of the human psyche has been widely recognized as an important framework for studying psychological problems. But he himself remarked that he could not claim to have reached any definite theory and that his work consisted of a series of different approaches. However, he did not apologize for this – he said that it was not possible to make up a simple formula to describe human nature because the psyche is so complex. By his own admission his ideas are not always easy to follow and so wading through the 20-volume collection of his work is not an easy task. This book provides a general introduction to both Jung and his work, and the section at the end, **Taking it further**, suggests ways in which you can continue your study of this fascinating and great thinker.

Summary

- Jung is famous because he founded a new system of psychology that he called analytical psychology.
- He regarded the spiritual and the numinous to be the most important aspects of his work and maintained that the psyche was as real as the external world.
- Jung coined the term 'analytical psychology' around 1913 in order to describe his work and to distinguish it from the system of psychoanalysis developed by Freud.

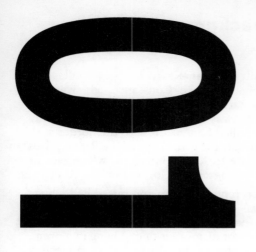

01

Jung's life and career

In this chapter you will learn:
- about Jung's family and social background
- key facts about his career
- details about his personal life and character.

Jung's family background

Nature

Jung was born on 26 July 1875 in Kesswil, a small village in Switzerland on the shores of Lake Constance. He was the second child born to his parents, but their first born had died soon after birth. When he was six months old, Jung's family moved to another village called Laufen, close to the border with Germany and France and near the great Falls of the Rhine. Then they moved again, this time to Klein-Hüningen, which was at that time just a village, near Basel, also located on the Rhine.

The little villages in which Jung was born and raised had a huge influence on him that was to last throughout his life. It was a peaceful, rural world of mountains and lakes, rocks, rivers and abundant wildlife. His earliest memory is one of lying in a pram, under the shadow of a tree on a warm summer's day, and feeling a great sense of glorious beauty and indescribable well-being on seeing the sunlight glittering through the leaves and blossoms. Jung developed an intense love of the natural world and a deep spiritual relationship with all living things. He loved the peace and solitude that living in nature can bring, and spent a lot of time alone thinking, writing, contemplating, and finding his own inner peace. His deep connection with the earth element was also expressed in painting pictures and working with wood and stone. Animals were very important to him – he always liked to have dogs as companions, and he frequently wrote of synchronous messages that came to him from the natural world.

When Jung was nine, his sister Gertrude was born, but she played little part in his childhood. The age gap between them was too great and their temperaments were very different. Young Carl was already a solitary child and liked to play alone, lost in his own inner world. Gertrude was delicate and died quite young. Jung said that she was always a stranger to him, and that where he was emotional she was always very composed, although she was very sensitive deep down.

Religion

Jung had many relations in the Church – in fact, his father and eight of his uncles were pastors, so religion must have had a huge influence on his childhood. His paternal grandfather – after whom he was named, Carl Gustav Jung (1794–1864) – was a respected physician and became Rector of Basel

University and Grand Master of the Lodge of Freemasons. He was rumoured to have been an illegitimate son of the great writer Goethe. On the other side of the family, Jung's maternal grandfather, Samuel Preiswerk (1799–1871), was a theologian who had a great interest in the occult. He held conversations with the dead and was given to visions; in her youth Jung's mother had often had to sit behind him when he was writing a sermon in order to prevent the devil from peering over his shoulder!

Jung's father was a pastor in the Swiss Reformed Church, whose teachings were strongly influenced by the sixteenth-century Reformation teachings of leaders such as Calvin and Luther. The Reformed Church taught people to believe in the literal truth of the Bible, or else risk damnation. Its teachings were strongly male dominated and puritanical – sex was regarded as a necessary evil at best, and women were generally despised and treated with suspicion.

These attitudes were strong and entrenched in society. When he was six young Carl was taken to a museum in Basel and was so fascinated by the stuffed animals he saw that the museum was being locked up before his aunt could tear him away. They had to go out by a different route from the one they had entered by, through the gallery of antiquities. Here he was mesmerized by beautiful figures, the like of which he had never seen before. His aunt was shocked to the core however, and dragged him away, telling him to close his eyes and not to be so disgusting – it was only then that it dawned on him that the figures were naked apart from fig leaves!

Parsons were very poorly paid at this time, and Jung's family lived the life of frugal poverty that was expected of loyal servants of God. The house he lived in as a small boy was a sombre eighteenth-century parsonage. The only man-made things of beauty he remembered from these early years were two paintings that hung in a dark room, set apart from everyday life. One was David and Goliath, the other a landscape of Basel dating from the early nineteenth century. Often he would creep into the room and sit for hours gazing at them. One cannot imagine a modern child, living in our busy world of constant over-stimulation, giving them more than a cursory glance, but for the young Carl they were a catalyst for a lifelong appreciation of art.

Jung's father had strong scholarly interests in Classical and Oriental studies, which probably also influenced Jung as he grew up, because he too studied the teachings of the East with great interest. Despite these interests however, and despite the fact that he lost his faith in God at an early stage, Jung's father accepted the teachings of his church and clung to them to the letter without question. Jung said later in life that in childhood he associated the word 'father' with reliability, but also with weakness. Perhaps he was already intuitively beginning to understand that such a dogmatic view of life is often used to cover up feelings of inadequacy and self-doubt. He came to see the male-dominated religion of his father as unbalanced, because it lacked the important feminine element which he later discovered in the teachings of Eastern religions. Jung's recognition of the danger of this kind of unbalanced view is enormously important and still has a clear message for the modern world.

Jung's mother was also rooted in the faith of the Reformed Church. However, her beliefs were more complex because her own family firmly believed in contact with the spirit world. Old pagan beliefs still held strong in the minds of people in rural Switzerland. Jung saw his mother as a dynamic and powerful person, but also rather unpredictable and mysterious. His parents' marriage was not an easy one, probably because their characters and beliefs were so very different. His mother was earthy, extrovert and chatty, whereas his father was a scholarly introvert. When Jung was three his mother was hospitalized for several months with a nervous illness, which he later said was no doubt caused partly by marital problems. During this time he was taken care of by a spinster aunt who was some 20 years older than his mother. He was deeply disturbed by his mother's absence and, as a result, for a long time associated the word 'love' with feelings of mistrust and the word 'woman' with unreliability.

Jung later revised his early childhood impressions of men and women, finding that he sometimes trusted men who turned out to be unreliable, and conversely found some women to be reliable despite his initial feelings of mistrust. Recognizing and overcoming unhelpful world views formed in early childhood is a part of the life work of the human psyche that is such an important part of Jung's teaching. (For more about the journey of the psyche, see Chapter 05.)

A brief outline of Jung's career

School

Jung attended a country school where he was intellectually well ahead of his classmates. He welcomed the company of other children, but close friendships were not easy for him because he was so used to playing alone. From the age of 11 he attended a school in Basel, but he was never happy there. The other boys thought him peculiar and tended to make fun of him. Not only that, but he found the lessons boring and felt that they were a waste of his time.

University

Family poverty meant that Jung could not expect to study at a more distant university, so he was admitted to Basel. He had originally wanted to study archaeology, but it was not taught at Basel, so he did medicine instead. This was in the family already as his paternal grandfather had been Professor of Surgery at the university. After obtaining his degree in medicine with a distinction in 1900, he almost decided to specialize in surgery, but he had developed a strong interest in psychiatry and eventually decided to move in this direction. This was a controversial direction to take, because psychiatry was the least-respected speciality in medicine at the time, but for Jung it was the perfect choice because it enabled him to study both the scientific and spiritual aspects of life.

First appointments

In 1900 Jung became an assistant at the Burghölzli mental hospital, a clinic attached to the University of Zürich. Jung worked under Eugen Bleuler (1857–1939), who was one of the most eminent psychiatrists of the day. In 1902 he was awarded his Ph.D. from the University of Zürich, and by 1905 he had been appointed lecturer in psychiatry and made Senior Staff Physician at Burghölzli.

Jung was especially interested in the disorder then called dementia praecox but later referred to as schizophrenia. He was fascinated by trying to find out what actually goes on in the minds of the mentally ill – for him their associations, dreams, hallucinations and gestures were not just 'mad', but full of important symbolic meaning. During this period he did a lot of research into word association. Most of his colleagues disagreed and took the firm **reductionist** stance that was popular at the time, tending to break everything down, including highly complex ideas, into simple component parts, so that everything was seen as working rather like a machine. This was held to be the scientific way of looking at things, but for Jung this was not a satisfactory method for exploring the human mind – it was too simplistic and did not allow for individuality.

In 1907 Jung published some of his observations in *The Psychology of Dementia Praecox,* thus enhancing his growing reputation as a research psychiatrist. He left the hospital in 1909 to concentrate on his work with private patients, and to give more time to his research into the psychological aspects of behaviour and the inner world of the unconscious.

Recognition of his importance

In 1907 Jung met Sigmund Freud in Vienna. Jung had become interested in Freud's concept of **repression** – a process of banishing unpleasant or undesirable feelings into the unconscious – an idea that seemed to corroborate some of Jung's own findings from his experiments in word association. In particular Jung was interested in Freud's work with dreams in relation to the repression process. Freud's ideas were unpopular at the time, but Jung risked his own reputation by backing Freud, and for a number of years there was a close friendship between them. Jung became the first president of Freud's International Psychoanalytic Association and was the editor of its journal, which was the first of its kind. In 1909 Jung travelled with Freud to lecture at Clark University at Worcester, Massachusetts in the USA and received an honorary degree.

Eventually Jung's independent way of thinking led to a rift with Freud in 1913. Following this rift Jung resigned from his presidency of the International Psychoanalytic Association, and then fell into a state of psychic depression and disorientation, at times verging on psychosis. This state was to haunt him for the next five or six years. He found it difficult to cope with everyday life, but he was determined to confront whatever was emerging from his unconscious. For a time he gave up public appearances, and even his academic career, resigning his lectureship at Zurich in order to concentrate on his self-analysis. Interestingly, the work he did on himself during this dark time was to lead him to some of his most important insights (see Chapter 03). In fact, he later said that all his work, all his creative activity, stemmed from dreams and fantasies that came to him during this period.

Jung saw military service in 1918 as Commandant at Chateaux d'Oex, a camp for British interns. During this time he began drawing mandalas, which are archetypal symbols found in many religions and other aspects of many cultures. These helped him to understand his psychic transformations from day to day and to emerge at last from his period of inner darkness (see pages 40–2). From 1918 until 1926 he studied the Gnostic writers, philosophers who lived during the period 100AD–300AD and were concerned with occult mystical knowledge and the world of the unconscious. However, in the end Jung decided they were too remote to form a real link with his current work.

Jung continued to develop his own school of psychology. After the First World War he travelled widely and studied the cultures and beliefs of tribal communities in places such as America, Africa and India. In 1928 he began reading alchemical texts and found concepts in them that excited him enormously because they confirmed many of his own ideas about how the human psyche transforms and develops. Here, at last, was the link he had been searching for, connecting the past and Gnosticism to the future and modern psychology. He researched alchemical studies for many years before finally publishing some of his findings in the 1930s and 1940s.

In 1936, when Harvard University marked its tercentenary by awarding honorary degrees to the most eminent living scientists, Jung was one of the people chosen. During the 1930s he also received doctorates from Oxford, two universities in Switzerland and three in India. His reputation had grown gradually and he had become a leader of international research work in psychology, partly because he eagerly exchanged ideas with others.

In 1933, Jung became president of the General Medical Society for Psychotherapy, an organization based in Germany, which was soon to be heavily influenced by Nazi thinking. Jung became increasingly uncomfortable about this emphasis and his link to the organization, coupled with work that he was currently doing about racial theories of the unconscious, led to widespread criticism and accusations of anti-Semitism. In 1939 he finally resigned from the organization (see Chapter 10).

In 1943 Jung was made Professor of Medical Psychology at the University of Basel, but the following year he suffered a heart attack and had to retire from his post. But he was still busy thinking and writing – many of his most important works were written during the years that followed. Even in old age he was still known as a great conversationalist, able to have informed discussions about a wide range of different topics. His charismatic personality meant that he attracted a huge following, but after his wife died in 1955 he began to shy away from the public eye until he died in 1961.

Jung's private life and personality

Jung, like most of us, was a man with contradictory sides to his personality. When a portrait of him was made in the 1930s by an anonymous woman, he said that it was not quite right, and that indeed it would be extremely difficult to get it right, because his spirit was not apparent in his external appearance. In fact he saw himself as a 'clash of opposites'. From early childhood Jung had observed similar conflicting characters in his mother. Emilie Jung, neé Preiswerk, was a large, kindly, motherly figure – she was a good cook and a ready listener, and had hidden literary talent. But there was another mother, an uncanny figure, who seemed to emerge at night. This mother was mysterious and ruthless, rather frightening in fact, and represented a more primitive kind of person altogether.

Despite the apparent maternal capability of his mother, Jung never felt particularly close to her and seems to have been reluctant to confide in her fully. Young Carl was a sensitive child and soon picked up on the ongoing conflict between his parents. This conflict was reflected in his inner world later on in life, as he struggled to reconcile the very different world views presented to him by his parents. From childhood onwards he saw himself as having two different aspects to his personality, which he labelled Number 1 and Number 2. (For more about this see Chapter 02.) His own complex psychological make-up is very much reflected in his theories of psychology, which are frequently concerned with the integration of opposites to make a meaningful whole. People who knew him well also observed that there seemed to be two different Jungs. On the one hand there was the modern, intellectual Jung, who drove around Zürich in a red car and grappled with problems of the psyche in his book-lined study. On the other hand there was the primitive Jung, who built himself a medieval-looking, fairy-tale tower by the lake at Bollingen. Here he would retreat in his spare time, living close to nature, crafting wood and stone, cooking, and doing his washing by hand. He would play for hours out of doors, tinkering with stones and water. Some people saw this as very odd behaviour for a distinguished professor.

Jung was always full of zest and enthusiasm, whatever he was doing: he was renowned for his loud wholehearted laugh. He was an open person too, always expressing his feelings both with his friends and in everyday life, and quite willing to admit to his own shortcomings. The down side to this openness was a foul temper which, on occasion, burst forth. Aniela Jaffé, his friend and administrative secretary describes how difficult this could be to cope with at times, but generously attributes it to his bossy Leo temperament and his extreme sensitivity, both of which enriched and burdened his life.

Jung's physical appearance matched his personality – he was tall and well built and many people found him physically attractive, especially women. He met his wife, Emma Rauschenbach (1882–1955) when he was just 21 and she was 16. The first time they met she was standing at the top of a staircase, and Jung had an immediate premonition that she was to be his wife. They were indeed married seven years later, in 1903, and their first child Agathe was born in 1904. Over the next ten years they had four more children, three more girls and a boy: Gret (born 1906), Franz (born 1908), Marianne (born 1910) and Helene (born 1914).

The children were given a liberal upbringing for the times. They were raised as Christians, but Jung also taught them different religious ideas, told them stories that fired their imaginations and encouraged them to find their own career paths. He allowed time to play with them, particularly while the family was on holiday. They often slept in tents, gathering their own firewood and water from the lake, and messing about in boats. Jung also encouraged their creativity using the natural resources of water, wood and stone that he loved himself.

At first the growing family lived in rooms at the Burghölzli hospital, but in 1909 they were able to move into a newly built house on the lakeside at Kusnacht near Zürich. Jung had known from very early childhood that he wanted to live near a lake. Luckily for him, Emma was a woman of substance, the daughter of a wealthy businessman, so this left Jung free to pursue his own interests a lot of the time.

Emma Jung worked as an analyst in the therapy practice, taking on her own patients. She also gave lectures at the Jungian institute in Zürich. She was especially interested in Arthurian legends, and made a special study of the Grail Legend. Antonia Wolff also worked alongside Jung and became his mistress from about 1911 onwards. The relationship between Jung and his two women became a complex triangular one that must have been very difficult for both the women. Jung himself was happy with it and fatly announced that a man needed two women – one to organize the domestic affairs and one to be stimulating to the intellect! In fact he was quite a womaniser and had various other affairs in addition to his relationship with Antonia.

Jung outlived both his beloved women and missed them in his last years. He carved memorial stones for each of them, with Chinese inscriptions. Emma's said, 'she was the foundation of my house' and Toni's said, 'she was the fragrance of the house'. He never wrote a great deal about people who were close to him, probably mainly in order to protect them.

Jung travelled extensively, visiting places as far apart as North Africa, New Mexico, East Africa (Kenya and Uganda) and India. He lectured in both Britain and America. People usually described Jung as being friendly and interested, but he had odd moods when he would become preoccupied, even rude. At these times he would withdraw from society and escape to his tower at Bollingen. When the mood took him he was totally driven by the need to indulge in creative activity or study, which meant that he sometimes hurt people or made enemies because he appeared distant.

All his life Jung had a strong belief in God, and insisted that regaining a religious attitude was the ultimate challenge for everyone. But he rejected dogma and fixed religious views, saying that understanding God had nothing to do with going to church or sticking to a particular creed. In his view, God needs mankind in order to mirror his creation and help it to unfold and grow. But rather than God being totally in charge, this is a two-way process, with man as co-creator. Jung saw a person's task in life as being the integration of the self, and the reconciliation of opposites in the psyche. He strongly emphasized the importance of myth, which appears in all cultures throughout recorded history, because it can act as a guide to show us the evolutionary path we are supposed to follow.

Jung died in 1961 after a brief illness. All his life he had been interested in the connections between what we think of as the 'outer' world and our own inner energy. For him all things had life – he was even known to give names to his pots and pans. He had lived in what many people saw as two separate worlds – the practical, earth-rooted world of nature, and the mysterious, numinous world of spirit. Nowadays many people recognize that the two worlds are actually part of a great whole, as modern physics and **esoteric** psychology are beginning to bridge the apparent gap. Many of Jung's ideas that seemed odd at the time are now beginning to make a lot of sense.

Summary

- Jung's early religious upbringing and his great love of nature particularly influenced his later thinking.
- He saw himself as having two personalities, one analytical and the other intuitive. From this he came to realize that integration of the different facets of the personality is an important life task.
- Although he was often regarded as an eccentric, Jung gradually acquired a huge following and became famous all over the world.
- He was a charismatic man, but at times he could be moody and difficult to live with.

02

Jung's early life

In this chapter you will learn:
- in more depth about Jung's childhood and early career
- about some major influences on his thinking
- the background to Jung's important relationship with Freud.

Boyhood

In his autobiographical book, *Memories, Dreams, Reflections*, which was written near the end of his life, Jung recalls various important incidents from his childhood. Some of these were to have profound effects upon his later thinking and haunt him all his life. From very early childhood he particularly remembered scenes that occurred in the nearby cemetery, where men would arrive dressed in long, black frock coats and tall hats, carrying a black box. His father would speak in a solemn voice, women would weep, and then they would bury someone in the ground. Understandably, when young Carl was told that Lord Jesus had taken these buried people to himself, he developed a great mistrust of Jesus. At about the same time in his childhood he encountered a Jesuit priest, whose sombre black-robed figure terrified the boy. He began to associate religion with feelings of fear and foreboding, and consequently began to hate going to church.

Because Jung played alone a great deal when he was a child, he became introspective and developed a rich and imaginative inner world. His later work as an analyst and a great thinker had its roots here. Young Carl spent a lot of time pondering philosophical and religious questions, many of which were very sophisticated for his age. His country playmates and other children he began to encounter at school were fun to be with, but he felt that they alienated him from his true self – he was only able to be truly himself when he played alone. He found his games totally absorbing and could not bear to be observed by other people. When he was with other children he would behave in a very different way, joining in their pranks, and even making up some of his own, which he never felt the need to do at home.

A childhood friend describes the young Carl as being very antisocial and quite unlike any other child he had met. When he and Carl were left alone to play together, Carl totally ignored him, absorbed in a game of ninepins all by himself in the middle of the room. Later in life, Jung remarked that he felt he needed people both more and less than others did. He found people fascinating, but he also needed a lot of personal space.

Jung's earliest recollected dream

When he was three or four, Jung dreamed that he was in a meadow not far from home, where he came upon a dark, stone-lined hole with steps leading down underground. He went down, hesitantly and full of fear, until he came to a doorway, closed off by a green curtain. Pushing this aside he entered a large underground chamber where there was a wonderful golden throne. Seated upon this throne was a huge thing made of flesh, 4.5–5.5 m high and about half a metre thick. On top it had a rounded head, with a single eye gazing upwards. He was paralysed with terror and, as he stood transfixed, he heard his mother's voice telling him, 'that is the man-eater'. At this point he woke up, terrified and sweating.

It was only years later that Jung realized that the huge thing of flesh was a phallus. The dream was oddly un-childlike and sophisticated – where had the anatomically correct phallus, sitting on a throne like some subterranean god, come from? Eventually he connected his dream with a book he read about the motif of cannibalism underlying the symbolism of the Christian Mass ceremony. He realized that the phallus in his dream was a ritual phallus, similar to those encountered in ancient religions. He was puzzled as to how a child could have had knowledge of such esoteric matters – things that were to fill his later years with 'stormiest passion'. Jung maintained that his intellectual life had its unconscious beginnings when he had that dream.

The stone

When he was aged between seven and nine, Jung often played near a wall made of large blocks of stone. He had a fascination for starting little fires in hollows in this wall. He felt that the fires were in some way sacred, and had to be kept fed so that they would burn forever. In front of the wall was a slope, with a stone in it that jutted out so that you could sit on it. Jung would play a game where he would alternate between being himself sitting on the stone, and being the stone which was being sat upon. After a while he would become uncertain of reality and would stand up wondering 'who was what now'. This confusion was exciting and interesting, and was always accompanied by 'a feeling of curious and fascinating darkness'. This was one of his first experiences of the numinous, which was to become of paramount importance to him in later years. The stone, in fact, was to become one of the foundations of his analytical psychology.

The secret manikin

Gradually, Jung began to be aware that he had two personalities, which he privately called 'Number 1' and 'Number 2'. The very different influences from his parents probably had a lot to do with creating this dualism in Jung's psyche.

- Number 1 was the socially adapted part of him, concerned with dutifully coping with the external, everyday world as best as he could. This side of Jung was ambitious and analytical, looking at the world from a scientific point of view and studying things by breaking them down into their separate elements.

- Number 2 was much older, secretive and mysterious and tended to look at things in an **intuitive** way, knowing things without having to reason them out. This was the part of him that felt close to nature and to God. This inward-looking aspect of his psyche felt essentially more real to him.

Jung clearly felt this duality in himself from an early age. When he was about ten, he carved a 5 cm manikin from the end of a ruler. The manikin wore a frock coat, top hat and shiny black boots. Jung sawed him off and made him a home in a wooden pencil case, complete with a little bed for him to lie on. He added a smooth black stone from the River Rhine, which he painted to divide it into upper and lower halves. The manikin and his sacred stone were secret and he knew that they somehow represented aspects of himself. Jung hid them on a beam in an attic where he was forbidden to play because the floorboards were unsafe.

Whenever he was upset or there was an undercurrent of trouble between his parents, Jung would sneak up to look at the manikin. Each time he visited, he added a tiny scroll, written upon in a secret language and bearing an important message. The secret manikin gave him a sense of power and security that was so important that he considered them to be the 'essential factor' of his boyhood. He knew that they represented an enormously important secret and that this was his first real attempt to give shape to it. Nobody could discover this secret and destroy it, and as long as his secret was safe, the tormenting sense of being divided into two warring halves was gone.

Much later, Jung saw his whole life as an unfolding of 'the self-realization of the unconscious'. He felt that what he referred to as a person's 'personal myth' could express that person's inner world more precisely than science ever could. The manikin in the attic was somehow symbolic of own inner world as a child – it was a part of his own evolving personal myth. As an adult Jung came to realize that this kind of duality and conflict exists in all of us and that our life's journey involves discovering and integrating the suppressed aspects of our psyche. But as he was growing up the conflict between his two opposing selves was very difficult, and he felt that he had to keep parts of his true self hidden. He later found parallels in the beliefs of ancient tribal people such as the Australian Aborigines and although in old age Jung's recollections of events in the external world faded, his encounters with the 'other reality' were as vivid as ever. These were what really mattered to him and he seems to have been aware of this from an early age.

The fantasy castle

As an adolescent Jung indulged, for some months, in an elaborate fantasy as he walked to school in Basel. This was a vision of a wonderful world where he would be totally in charge. There was no school in this world – instead he lived in a castle on a rocky island in the middle of a lake. This could only be accessed by a narrow isthmus, and even that was cut off from the mainland by a broad canal with a wooden bridge over it. The castle had a tall keep and was surrounded by a medieval city, ruled by a mayor and a council of old men. Carl himself was justice of the peace, arbitrator and advisor, and he only came out in public occasionally in order to hold court. The most important part of the fantasy was an amazing secret that only he knew about. The tower of the keep contained a vast copper column or cable as thick as a man's arm, which extended right from the battlements down into the cellars. At the top were masses of fine filaments extending into the air, which extracted a mysterious spiritual essence from the atmosphere. This was drawn down the copper column into the cellar and transformed into gold. The existence of this process was a vital secret that had to be concealed from the council of elders and even, in a sense, from himself.

This fantasy illustrates the almost unbearable loneliness and isolation that Jung felt during his childhood and adolescence. The tall keep of the castle, almost impossible to reach on its rocky island, shows how he protected his hidden self. He was a deeply spiritual child and yet he was unable to talk to anyone about any of his spiritual experiences – in fact, they had to be kept totally secret like the manikin in his hidden attic. The mysterious copper column, carrying out its hidden process of transformation seems to foreshadow his later fascination with alchemy.

Education

School

In 1886, when Jung was 11, he began secondary school in Basel. Here, for the first time, he was among wealthier people and began to be aware of a deep sense of envy. He was seen by other children as a bit odd and unpredictable and was not particularly popular. Teachers found him frustrating too, because he seemed to be very clever when his interest was held, but he refused to compete with his classmates and was sometimes disruptive and made himself appear stupid. Whenever anything went wrong, the finger of blame always seemed to be pointed at him and he was seen as a troublemaker, but in fact he was just being used as a scapegoat. Eventually, when he was 15, a gang of seven boys lay in ambush and attacked him, but he was big and strong by then and, seized by one of his violent rages, he picked up one of the boys by both arms and swung him at the others, knocking several of them off their feet. After that he was left alone!

Jung describes having an early personal insight into the process of forming a neurosis, which developed as a result of his feelings of alienation. When he was 12 years old he was pushed over by another boy and banged his head. Even as he fell he heard an inner voice telling him that this would be a good excuse not to have to go to school any more. After that he began to have fainting fits whenever school or work were mentioned. He was kept off school for six months and enjoyed rambling around alone, living with nature and communing with his inner world, but all the time his pleasure was somewhat spoilt by a vague sense of guilt. Eventually, he overheard his father talking to a friend and telling him how worried he was about his son's future. He was afraid that he might be epileptic and consequently unable to support himself when he grew up. Jung rushed off and began to study his Latin books, struggling every few minutes to overcome giddy spells. Within a few weeks he was back at school and had the uncomfortable realization that he had engineered the whole neurotic episode himself. From

Maths was sheer terror and torture.

then on he worked hard. As he walked to school one day he suddenly felt as if he had emerged from a dense cloud. He thought to himself, 'now I am *myself*'.

Jung was nevertheless bored by school, feeling that it took up too much of his valuable time. Many subjects he found too easy and did very well in them. However, he objected strongly to algebra, because it proposed ideas that seemed to him to be downright lies, such as A = B, which was a bit like saying like saying sun = moon. In fact, he found maths as a whole to be 'sheer terror and torture'.

He had an 'utter incapacity' for drawing, and gymnastics was ruined for him by physical timidity and the fact that he resented people telling him how to move. This added to the enduring sense of inferiority he suffered as he grew up, feeling himself to be somehow contemptible. Divinity he found 'unspeakably dull', and he was still suspicious of the 'Lord Jesus' he was taught about at home and at school. His father's religious instruction to prepare him for confirmation bored him horribly, but he was becoming increasingly fascinated by the concept of God and other religious questions. Here he sensed an unfathomable mystery, the existence of a unique being who was impossible to understand. He tried to discuss these matters with his father, but felt that his father merely repeated to him what he himself had learned, and had no real depth of understanding at all. His father emphasized that all one had to do was to have faith and that too much thinking was dangerous. Young Carl disagreed, and felt that it was important to experience things for oneself in order to find the truth.

Ideas about God

When he was about 12 years old Jung had an experience that was to change his whole attitude to religion. He was walking home from school one gloriously sunny day and saw the roof of the cathedral glittering as the sun shone on the newly glazed tiles. This made him think about how beautiful the world was, and a moment later he was suddenly swamped by an overwhelming feeling of guilt, and he told himself to stop thinking immediately, in case an appalling thought popped into his head and made him commit a frightful sin. He arrived home feeling very worked up, and that night and for the next two nights his sleep was restless and disturbed to such an extent that his mother thought he must be ill. On the third night he awoke sweating with fear, convinced that God was testing him and trying to force him to think something wicked. Finally he could stand it no longer, and mustering all his psychic strength he willed the dreaded thought to emerge. Then he saw a vision of the cathedral, the blue sky and God sitting above it all on his golden throne, and suddenly, to his amazement, a huge turd fell from under the throne and smashed the whole cathedral to pieces!

Allowing this thought finally to emerge brought Jung an indescribable feeling of relief. He had finally yielded to God's command and allowed himself to think the unthinkable. Now, of course, there emerged a difficult question – why should God want to befoul his own cathedral in this way? Gradually there came a dim understanding that perhaps there was another aspect to God, a side of him that could be negative and terrible. Years later Jung was to develop this idea much further in his writing, for example in his book *Answer to Job*. Looking back late in his life, he saw this experience as being of fundamental importance to his whole understanding of the nature of God.

Young Carl was surrounded by people who supposedly knew all about spiritual matters and he frequently listened to their conversations, but all the time he wondered to himself 'What about the secret?' He always felt that there was some hidden secret of grace about which his father and uncles knew nothing. Church gradually became a torment to him as he sat and listened to men who presumed to preach aloud about the nature of God, as if they knew what were his real intentions and actions. For him the concept of the reality of God could not be expressed with stale words and rituals. He also felt guilty because he alone had grasped the dual nature of God and knew that God had a nasty side to his nature that wanted him to do things that were wrong.

In vain Jung searched through his father's library, reading anything he felt might enlighten him further about the nature of God, but even there he found no answers. His only comfort was to sit upon his stone and ponder on the fact that the stone had no uncertainties and stayed eternally the same for thousands of years without experiencing all the angst and emotion that coursed through him. This thought was strangely calming and reassuring.

Between the ages of 16 and 19 Jung's lengthy sense of depression slowly lifted, but he was still rather unpopular with his schoolmates. He was still struggling with his feeling of an inner split in his personality, which seemed to force him to try and live in two very different worlds at once. Partly because of this he felt unable to decide what to study at university. He was fascinated by natural science – zoology, palaeontology and geology – but felt equally drawn to comparative religion and prehistoric archaeology. Eventually, in 1895, he won a scholarship and went to Basel University to study medicine.

His 'Number 2' personality faded for the time being into the background as Jung became occupied with his studies and new social life. Being at University made him really feel alive and he made plenty of friends. He became an avid scholar, reading books on philosophy as well as medicine, and great works of literature such as Goethe's *Faust*. He joined the university debating society where they talked about the human soul and other interesting religious questions. His interest in psychic phenomena deepened as he read work by writers such as Swedenborg (1688–1772 – theologian, scientist and philosopher) and discovered reports of psychic events in cultures from all over the world.

Jung stopped going to church and had a lot of arguments with his father, who became increasingly depressed and died of cancer during Jung's first year at Basel. His father's death seemed to change Jung's whole personality and he became known as 'the Barrel'. Suddenly he became loud and sociable, going to parties and dances, sometimes getting drunk, and falling hopelessly and inappropriately in love.

Scientific thinking at the turn of the last century

In the 1890s, when Jung was a student, psychiatry was in its infancy. People tended to see it as being related to psychical research and spiritualist ideas. These were very much in vogue at the time, and the Society for Psychical Research had been founded in 1882 in Cambridge, England. At the same time new scientific understanding of the unconscious was beginning to emerge, pioneered by Sigmund Freud. The accepted way of thinking in science was based on **positivism**, which limits knowledge to things that are directly observable. This approach goes hand in hand with the mechanistic view, which says that everything is determined by strictly physical or chemical processes.

The idea behind positivism is simple – you describe the facts of what you can experience and observe. Anything else is not considered to be science. Positivists also try to make general scientific laws about the ways in which phenomena are related. This approach began in the natural sciences and spread into philosophy. Most psychologists took the positivist stance, but psychiatry was also developing at this time, as people became interested in mental illnesses that were hard to explain by means of contemporary medicine and mechanistic thinking.

Jung was aware, even before he turned to psychiatry as his main field of study, that his way of thinking was going to be different from the mainstream and that this independence of thought would at times lead him into frightening isolation. Soon after he began his studies at Basel he had a dream. It was night-time and he was struggling through a dense fog, battling with a mighty wind. His hands were cupped around a tiny light which he had to protect from going out. He had a horrible sense of being followed, and glancing behind him saw a gigantic black figure. This filled him with terror, but he realized that as long as he kept the tiny light alive everything would be all right. When he woke up he recognized the huge black figure as the Brocken Spectre, an optical illusion sometimes seen in mountainous areas, where a vast shadow of the observer is cast onto a bank of mist, looking for all the world like a gigantic black ghost. Jung realized that this spectre was his own shadow, cast by the tiny flickering light that he carried. This light was the light of his own unconscious, which was the only light he had and also the greatest treasure he possessed.

While he was at Basel, Jung joined a student society called the Zonfingia Society, and began to put across some of his unusual ideas. The first paper he presented to the society, called *On the Limits of the Exact Sciences,* attacked the materialist limitations of current scientific thinking. Later, he suggested that the human soul could be a suitable subject for scientific study even though it existed outside what were perceived as the boundaries of the normal physical world. He suggested that more could be discovered about the soul through studying mediums, hypnosis and phenomena such as sleep walking.

Jung's interest in spiritualism

Jung was so interested in the idea of studying psychic phenomena of this kind that he decided to make them the subject of his doctoral thesis. He came upon a small book on spiritualism and realized that the phenomena described were related to stories that were familiar from his country childhood and tales that had been related to him about members of his family. Such things as predictive dreams, clocks that stopped at the moment of death, ghosts and table turning fascinated him. His friends, on the other hand, reacted to such ideas either with total disbelief or with defensiveness, even dread.

When he was home for the summer holidays, an incident occurred that affected Jung profoundly. The family heard a loud crack from the dining room. Rushing through, they found that their circular walnut dining table had split right across the middle, not along a joint, but clean through the solid wood. A few weeks later another deafening cracking sound was traced to a bread knife, which lay inside the sideboard shattered into several pieces along the blade. The knife had been used at teatime and then put away as normal.

Jung and his mother both felt that there must be some underlying reason for these two strange incidents. A few weeks later he was asked to attend a seance and he decided to go along, thinking that the incidents might be somehow to do with the medium. After that he attended regular seances on Saturday evenings. The medium, Hélène Preiswerk, was a young cousin of Jung's, and during seances she took on the personality of a woman called Ivenes. Through Ivenes she relived past life experiences and dramatic love affairs. Jung's doctoral thesis, *On the Psychology and Pathology of So-Called Occult Experiences*, used Hélène as a research subject. Eventually Jung lost interest when he discovered that the girl had falsified some of the evidence in order to impress him, but he felt that the whole experience had been important because it had further aroused his interest in the workings of the human psyche. Hélène's mediumistic ability had given him some insight into the nature of the unconscious mind. His fellow students teased him about his interest in occult phenomena, but he stuck to his guns and pursued his interest, studying spiritualistic literature and doing experiments in the field. It angered him that contemporary science refused to investigate such phenomena, choosing instead simply to deny their existence.

Jung realized that once more he was being pulled in two directions: science emphasized the investigation of concrete facts, whereas philosophy and comparative religion placed importance on the spiritual side of life. However, it seemed to Jung that both disciplines fell short of the truth: science was unable to give a sense of meaning, and religion lacked objective empiricism. For a long time he was unable to decide what to concentrate on in his studies, so he felt a great wave of excitement when he first came upon a book about psychiatry by Krafft-Ebing. Krafft-Ebing spoke of the subjective nature of psychiatry, describing how the psychiatrist studied his patients with the whole of his own personality. Jung realized with a flash of insight that here, at last, was a way in which he could integrate the two currents of his internal world. This was where science and the spiritual met. His decision to study psychiatry was met with disbelief and dismay by fellow students and tutors alike. Once again the age-old feeling of being an outsider returned, but this time he had more confidence and he knew that his chosen path was the right one for him.

Burghölzli

In 1900 Jung was appointed as an assistant at Burghölzli, a psychiatric clinic at the University of Zurich, run by Eugen Bleuler, who was one of the most eminent psychiatrists of the day. Jung was rapidly promoted to deputy director and also took a post as lecturer in psychiatry and psychotherapy at Zürich University. The patients at Burghölzli were mainly psychotic – that is, they suffered from the more severe mental disorders. Jung worked here for nine years, studying the group of illnesses then known as dementia praecox, now called schizophrenia. The mechanistic outlook said that such illnesses were caused by neurological damage or organic disease. Jung was not satisfied by this attitude, however, because all it really enabled the doctor to do was make rather meaningless diagnoses, describe symptoms, or compile statistics. The personality of the patient and his individuality did not seem to matter. But Jung was not interested in labelling people and he was quick to recognize that paranoid ideas and hallucinations actually contained hidden symbolic meaning, connected to the individual's life story.

Jung was especially interested in experimental psychology and did extensive work using word-association tests. This kind of test was originally devised by Sir Francis Galton, (1822–1911) and further developed by Wilhelm Wundt (1832–1920). Although it was considered somewhat old-fashioned, it was still being used, particularly with criminal cases. The idea was simple enough: the doctor gave the patient a list of a hundred or so words and the patient responded to each with whatever came first into his or her head. Response times were measured with a stop-watch and each response was noted down, then the whole list was repeated and the person had to give the same responses as the first time. Mistakes or noticeable delays suggested that unconscious emotions were probably at work. Jung found that he could identify what he called 'complexes' of related responses. These represented related groups of emotionally charged unconscious ideas, thoughts and images. For example, someone with a complex about money might show a disturbance in response to words such as 'buy', 'pay' or 'money'. When an old professor of criminology announced that he did not believe in the validity of the tests, Jung challenged him to try one himself. To his astonishment Jung was soon able to tell him that he had financial worries, was afraid of dying of heart disease and had long ago studied in France, where he had had a love affair! Jung had gathered all this information from the professor's responses to the words 'heart', 'death', 'to pay' and 'kiss'.

Jung also worked with a galvanometer, an electrical instrument that measures the electrical conductivity of the skin. This varies according to how damp the skin is – when a person is stressed it tends to be damper and the skin conducts electricity more easily. The galvanometer was therefore used as a sort of lie detector, and Jung actually managed to use this method to catch a nurse who had been stealing money. He later abandoned the idea of using a galvanometer because he realized that the stress level was more related to a person's *feelings* of guilt than to *actual* guilt.

Jung was interested in the psychogenic causes of mental illness. **Psychogenic disorders** are those that originate with mental conditions – physical symptoms are seen as secondary and not causative. For Jung, each patient has a story that needs to be told and this is where therapy should begin. A person's symptoms will often make perfect sense in the light of their individual story, and the problem must be seen in relation to the whole person, never to the symptom alone. Jung began to explore the unconscious minds of his patients, using word association, dream analysis, or simply by endlessly and patiently talking. Jung believed that psychotic symptoms were linked with toxic substances circulating in the blood, but he also suggested that the patient's energy was being withdrawn from the outer world and concentrated on the inner world where dreams, myths and fantasies held sway. In 1907 he wrote about his ideas and observations in *The Psychology of Dementia Praecox,* a study that added to his growing reputation as an up-and-coming figure in psychiatric research.

Meanwhile, Freud's new ideas about the unconscious were beginning to be heard by the scientific community. These suggested that Jung might be right in his suggestion that there were more factors at work in causing mental illness than the mechanistic approach had assumed. Freud had a theory that unwanted and uncomfortable ideas were banished from the conscious mind by a process he called repression. This idea seemed to Jung to be supported by what he had discovered in his word-association experiments. In 1906 Jung sent Freud a copy of his book, *Studies in Word Association,* as soon as it was published. Freud was most enthusiastic about it and invited Jung to go to Vienna to meet him. This was to be the beginning of a very important relationship between the two great men.

Jung and Freud

Jung was very heavily influenced by Freud and worked closely with him between 1907 and 1913. Freud's ground-breaking psychoanalytic therapy was aimed at treating mental and nervous disorders. It was new and different from accepted methods of dealing with mental illness, because it worked with theories about the unconscious and the ways in which it interacts with the conscious mind. The therapy was based partly on a free-association process very similar to Jung's work with word association. The patient was helped by this method to recall repressed experiences and so begin to come to terms with any underlying neurosis. Freud also worked a great deal with dreams, and this aspect of his work also greatly interested Jung.

Freud extended psychoanalysis to include a system of developmental psychology in which he described certain biologically determined phases that he believed everyone goes through during childhood. According to Freud, people can get stuck at any stage in the process and this causes problems later on in life, which often emerge in the form of neuroses. People tend to get stuck as a result of conflicts that arise between basic biological urges and the norms for correct behaviour imposed by society. For a long time Freud insisted that these basic urges were fundamentally sexual in nature. He used the term **libido** to describe the sexual drive that gave rise to the urges.

Freud and Jung got on especially well at first, and a kind of father-son relationship developed between them, Freud being nearly 20 years older than Jung. Freud wanted Jung to be his successor and in 1910 he appointed him as the President of the newly formed International Psychoanalytic Society. However, problems soon began to arise in their relationship. Freud found out that Jung had been having an illicit affair with one of his patients and he confronted Jung disapprovingly. Jung retaliated by being rather hostile towards Freud, who then claimed that Jung taunted him by talking incessantly about some mummified peat bog men that were being dug up in northern Germany. Jung connected these with other mummified remains that had been found in cellars at Bremen, where they were staying at the time. Perhaps he was implying that Freud's ideas were 'mummified'. Freud certainly seems to have felt that he was being taunted, because he became very upset and eventually fainted. Later, he explained that this was because he had felt that Jung had a death wish against him. He had hinted at this notion previously, when he had tried to analyze a dream of Jung's involving skeletons in a cellar (you can read more about this dream in Chapter 06).

Jung had always felt that Freud tended to put him on a pedestal. His own feelings were very intense too – he said that it was almost as if he had a teenage crush on Freud. Freud had also recognized that this intensity of feeling might end up in some sort of 'teenage rebellion'. Gradually this began to happen, as Jung began to formulate new theories of his own. He said that he had had reservations about Freud's ideas from the beginning, and this was in fact true – as early as 1906 he had stated that just because he acknowledged some of Freud's ideas that did not mean that he placed sexuality prominently in the foreground as Freud did. He added that Freud's method of therapy was not the only one available, and that perhaps it did not always prove as effective in practice as it appeared to be in theory. Neither was Jung convinced that positive results could be explained in quite the way that Freud suggested. Freud had a theory that the most important part of therapy was a process he called 'abreaction', when repressed emotions stemming from childhood sexual traumas were released from the unconscious. For Jung, things were not as cut and dried as this. He believed that people's neuroses were more to do with problems in their current life, albeit often linked to earlier traumas. He also suggested that the efficacy of Freud's methods could be partly to do with developing a personal rapport with the patient. One of the most important differences between Freud's and Jung's thinking was that Freud always tended to concentrate on a person's past, whereas Jung looked more to the present and the possible future.

Jung also disagreed with Freud about the problem of incest. Freud insisted that neurotic problems in adulthood were caused by repressed infantile desires of an incestuous nature, where the child desired a relationship with the parent of the opposite sex. This was what he called the Oedipus complex. For Jung this was far too simplistic. He did not believe that sexual fantasies of this sort were the cause of neurosis; rather, they arose from time to time as a result of a person's inability to adapt to present circumstances. He said that it was relatively rare for incest to cause personal complications, and insisted that in fact incest has a highly religious aspect which appears in many myths.

Jung knew that Freud would never be able to accept some of his ideas, and for a while he was tormented by a conflict between his urge to express himself and the risk of losing an important friendship. In 1912 he lectured at Fordham University in New York. Outwardly he was still struggling to be supportive of Freud, but in fact he ended up criticizing many of the basic theories of psychoanalysis, saying that:

- the 'libido' should not be regarded as merely sexual, but more as a universal life force. Later he abandoned this term altogether and tended to refer to 'psychic energy'
- pleasure could come from all sorts of non-sexual sources, not merely from sexual sources as Freud had tended to insist
- adult neuroses were caused by current problems that resurrected old conflicts. These were not necessarily infantile conflicts, nor were they always sexual.

Not long after this attack, Freud and Jung met up again at a conference in Munich in 1912. Freud talked to Jung at length and felt that he had won him back into the fold. Freud then proceeded to faint again at lunch, and Jung had to carry him through into another room. Clearly Freud was deeply upset about the whole affair. The next year, Jung lectured in London and talked once again about wanting to move psychoanalysis away from its narrow emphasis on sex. He coined the phrase 'analytical psychology' at this time to describe the new ideas that he was evolving and to distinguish them from psychoanalysis.

Letters between Freud and Jung became increasingly bitter and Jung accused Freud of behaving like a controlling father, intolerant towards new ideas. Sadly, in 1913 their friendship ceased altogether and before long Jung resigned his presidency of the International Psychoanalytical Society. In spite of this, there is no doubt that Freud was very important in helping Jung towards formulating his theories. You can read more about their relationship in *The Freud/Jung Letters* (see **Further reading** on page 155).

Summary

- Jung was a solitary child and in his imaginative games he began to grapple with some of the ideas that were to fascinate him all his life.
- School largely bored him and it was not until he discovered psychiatry that he began to find his true path in life.
- He had a lifelong interest in the paranormal, which was to have profound influences upon his work.
- His work at Burghölzli brought him into contact with psychotic patients and inspired his interest in the ways in which the human personality develops.
- Freud was a very important figure in the development of Jung's ideas.

03

Jung's inner world

In this chapter you will learn:
- how Jung's midlife crisis was vital to the development of his work
- the importance of listening to messages from the unconscious
- about Jung's retreat at Bollingen.

Jung's midlife crisis

After Jung had fallen out with Freud, he went into a lengthy period of great uncertainty that nowadays would probably be called a midlife crisis. Interestingly, Freud had also been through a similar inner crisis at about the same age. Such crises are quite common, especially after a prolonged period of intellectual activity, and seem to represent a kind of integration process, where the person stops to listen to what has been stored away in the unconscious and takes stock of everything that has been learned in life so far. The process can be very nurturing to creativity – both Freud and Jung published ground-breaking books soon after they recovered from their crises. Freud's was one of his best-known books, *The Interpretation of Dreams,* and Jung's was to be *Psychological Types,* published in 1921.

Jung was 39 when his crisis began. He had lost a lot of his former friends, his writing was not being well received, people were dismissing him as an airy-fairy mystic. Most of the academic world turned its back on him and he gave up his public positions, including his university post and his post with the Psychoanalytical Society. He felt a great sense of disorientation, as if he were suspended in midair and could not find his footing or his true path in life. But this was something he had seen coming for some time – he knew that his way of thinking was different and would eventually lead him to this difficult crossroads. His reaction was to turn away from the world for a while and withdraw into his own inner world. Up until now he had lived most of his adult life according to the characteristics of what he called his personality Number 1, with its worldly concerns of establishing his career, achieving academic success and so on. The Number 2 personality, with its dreams, visions and dark secrets, had been largely suppressed since adolescence, but now it demanded to be heard.

Dreams and fantasies became increasingly interesting to Jung as a huge torrent of them began to pour out of his unconscious, to the extent that he felt as if huge blocks of stone were tumbling down on him. He was not only interested in his own dreams and fantasies, but in those of his patients as well. He couldn't understand why other doctors were so obsessed with making firm diagnoses and did not seem interested in what their patients actually had to *say.* It became of paramount importance to him to develop a new attitude to his patients and stop bringing any preconceived theoretical premises to bear on their cases. As a result, he found that his patients would spontaneously tell him about their dreams and fantasies, and he would simply encourage them to explore them further by asking open-ended questions such as, 'Where does that come from?' or, 'What do you think about that?' He soon decided that he was right to respond in this way, because actually dreams and fantasies are the only material we have to work with when exploring the psyche. Looking back on his life's journey so far, he realized that this was a very important revelation. In giving dreams and fantasies this kind of importance he had hit upon a 'key to mythology' which would unlock the secrets of the human psyche.

The importance of mythology

Jung had been interested in mythology for many years. During his time working at Burghölzli he began to realize that many myth-like themes emerged in the dreams and fantasies of the insane. Current thinking in psychiatry said that people carried daily 'residues' – images from normal day-to-day experiences that were consciously forgotten but were stored away in the unconscious. Much of the contents of a neurosis could be explained by looking at stored fragments of this kind which sprang from events that had occurred in the patient's life. But many of Jung's psychotic patients produced imagery that was strikingly universal, and difficult to explain away merely as a product of the person's personal history and day-to-day experience. This imagery was often similar to that found in the kind of dream that people living in primal societies commonly called a 'big dream'. Jung began to wonder whether it was possible that alongside all the information collected from their own everyday lives, people also carried 'archaic residues', by which he meant little snippets of inherited impressions and imagery, stored in myth-like forms. From this idea he began to develop his theories about the collective unconscious, which he saw as the deepest layer of the unconscious, extending beyond the individual psyche. He realized that myths are important to all humans and that they seem to express these unconscious ideas in accessible story form.

Many of the images contained in myths are what Jung called 'archetypes', which are recurring images or patterns of thinking that represent typical human experiences. Nowadays we are familiar with this idea – most people understand what is meant by an 'archetypal father figure', for example. Jung began to see how mythology, archetypes and the collective unconscious were all linked together. He realized that myths were stories that helped people to understand common psychic processes and the ways in which the human psyche develops on its journey through life. Such ideas appear worldwide in fairy stories, mythology, and in the dreams and fantasies of both 'normal' people and those suffering from mental illness. Myths are healing to the psyche in a way that intellectual thought cannot be, because they connect us to the deeper levels of our being: they connect us to what Jung called an 'age-old animal power', and they give us a sense of religious experience. Myths arise from archetypes, which are not intellectually invented but are always there, forming the structure of the primordial collective unconscious.

During his period of crisis Jung found many references in literature to people who had undergone a similar confrontation with their own unconscious. He read about the shamanic soul quests of people in primal cultures, and stories of mythic heroes who went off on a 'Nekyia', or 'night-sea journey'. This was a very dangerous form of quest where the hero was likely to be swallowed up by vast sea monsters or by an all-devouring female. For Jung, this female figure seemed to represent the mother to whom we are normally attached in our childhood and from whom we must eventually separate our own psyche. Sometimes the hero has to be swallowed up by a monster in order to find re-birth. This mythical idea corresponded very closely with what was going on in Jung's own inner crisis. He seemed to live under a constant inner pressure, at times so strong that he thought he must have some serious psychic disturbance. But he also realized that the dreams and visions that were flooding through his troubled psyche were somehow connected to the ideas expressed in myths. They were the substance of what he called the **mythopoeic** imagination, which has tended to be overlooked in our rational age.

Such imaginative ideas are everywhere, but, as Jung had already discovered, they tend to be found mainly at the unconscious level and are often treated with dread and suspicion when they emerge into consciousness. Many people are scared of what goes on in their own unconscious and see any investigation as being dangerous – they are afraid that they might lose control. Indeed, Jung knew all too well from his clinical work how dangerous the unconscious could be, and at times he feared that he might become psychotic like his patients. He felt a huge resistance and an almost overwhelming sense of fear at the incessant flood of fantasies that was pouring out of his unconscious, but rather than trying to suppress them he surrendered himself to the process, trying desperately to understand what all the visions meant.

Jung noticed that mythical figures began to feature frequently in his dreams. One of these was Siegfried, a figure from Germanic myth. Siegfried was the archetypal hero who brandished a magical sword, slew dragons, discovered caves full of treasure and won the hand of a beautiful princess. Jung had long had a secret sense of identity with this hero, but in his dream he actually *killed* Siegfried. In the dream Jung found himself in a lonely, rocky landscape, with a brown-skinned stranger. It was early dawn and the eastern sky was already growing light. When Siegfried's horn sounded over the mountains, Jung knew that he and the stranger had to kill him. They lay in ambush with rifles, and when Siegfried appeared, driving at furious speed in a chariot made from the bones of the dead, they shot at him and killed him. A ghastly feeling of guilt flooded through Jung, but there was an immediate downpour of rain that he knew would erase all trace of their heinous deed.

Jung was at first unable to understand this dream, but he knew that it was imperative for him to do so – in fact, an inner voice told him that he must understand its message or else shoot himself. At last he grasped what it meant: Siegfried represented the urge to achieve in a heroic way, imposing his will upon others; the dream showed Jung that he had to look beyond the will of his **ego**, sacrificing his conscious ideals and attitudes, in order to surrender to the powerful messages of the unconscious.

Keeping his grip on reality was a real struggle for Jung at this time, and he realized that it was essential to maintain a normal life in the outer world in order to counterbalance his excursions into his inner world. His health suffered during his mental crisis and he went through periods of insomnia and stomach trouble. Fortunately, his family and his work acted as anchors, reminding him that he was a real person and preventing him from becoming totally ungrounded. Jung was determined that he would remain somehow in control, and began to study his own crisis almost as if he were both patient and doctor at the same time. He felt lost, without a frame of reference, and so he began to look around for ways to chart his journey.

Creative play

Jung tried going over all the details of his childhood in order to find a cause for his disturbances. He went through this process twice, but it seemed to get him nowhere, so in the end he decided that the only thing to do was to be less analytical and try submitting to the impulses of his own unconscious. This had interesting results. The first thing that came into his head seemed to be a memory of a passionate interest he had had when he was about ten years old. He had endlessly used building blocks to construct little houses, castles and villages. Later on he had used ordinary stones, with mud for mortar. As the memory welled up he felt very emotional and excited, and he realized that the small boy he had once been was still inside him somewhere, and possessed a creative life that his adult self lacked. He decided to re-enact the childish phase by indulging in similar games. In doing this Jung was one of the first to recognize the existence of the 'inner child' that is often encountered in modern therapies. At first he felt self-conscious and humiliated to be playing like a child, but he soon found that it was a good way of getting back in touch with the true essence of himself at that age.

Jung collected suitable stones and began to build. He made cottages, a castle, a village and a church, but he hesitated to add an actual altar within the church. Then, one day, walking by the

Jung would play every afternoon until his patients arrived.

lake, he found a perfect little red stone pyramid, about 4 cm high. He was delighted, realizing that this must be the altar for his church. As he put it in position he was reminded of the phallus dream he had had when he was very young – the strange god seated upon his underground throne. He felt immensely satisfied by this.

Every afternoon Jung would play until his patients arrived, and then again in the evening. Gradually, his thoughts clarified and he found that he was able to understand far more about his own psychic world. He developed an inner certainty that what he was doing was discovering his own myth. The building work acted like a trigger, releasing a whole stream of fantasies that he carefully wrote down. For the rest of his life he used such creative play as an invaluable therapeutic tool. Whenever he came up against a mental block he would paint, or work in stone, and he always found that this would get his ideas flowing again so that he could begin to write. Creative play was also to become a very important aspect of Jungian analysis.

Dreams, visions and fantasies

Jung found that patients would often report their dreams and fantasies to him spontaneously, and he would then ask them questions in order to try and unravel what they meant. Interpretations of the dreams and fantasies seemed to follow of their own accord; from the patients' replies and associations. Jung deliberately avoided all theoretical rules – he simply tried to help people to understand their own imagery.

Meanwhile, he was also fascinated by his own dreams and he spent a lot of time trying to interpret them, although this was sometimes very difficult. For example, he dreamed of a long row of corpses, each dressed in different clothes going back through the ages to a twelfth-century crusader dressed in chain mail. Each corpse in turn stirred and began to come to life as he looked at it. Jung realized that this particular dream was speaking to him about aspects of the unconscious that are handed down from the ancestors and can still stir and come to life in our own psyches. He felt that the dream tied in with the ideas that he was developing about archetypes and the collective unconscious.

In 1913, Jung began to feel his own immense inner pressure moving outwards, 'as though there were something in the air'.

The very atmosphere seemed darker, as if his inner oppression was becoming a concrete reality. During a journey, he had an overpowering vision of a huge flood that rose up and covered the whole of Northern Europe. The mountains rose higher to protect Switzerland, but all around he saw the rubble of civilization and drowned bodies in a vast sea that turned to blood. The whole vision lasted an hour and made him feel quite ill. Two weeks later it returned, with even more intensity.

This gruesome experience was followed by a recurring dream that began in the spring of 1914. In his dream, Jung saw the land frozen to ice in summer time. The First World War broke out in August, and Jung knew then that he had to try to understand how his own inner experiences had coincided with the outer experiences of mankind. He realized that the only way to approach this question was to begin to record carefully and study his own fantasies and dreams. He began by writing down ideas that came to him in the course of his creative play. A huge stream of fantasies began to be released and Jung felt that he 'stood helpless before an alien world'. This was hard to cope with and he felt as if he was enduring an endless series of inner thunderstorms. He knew that he was strong, however, and that he had to find meaning in it all, not only for his own sake, but also for the sake of his patients, so that he might better understand their problems. He went on struggling with his visions and writing everything down, often having to resort to yoga exercises to try and control his overwrought emotions. He knew that this work was of paramount importance and had to take precedence over everything else. He only did yoga until he felt calm, and then once more he would allow the visions and fantasies to have free reign. He realized that what he was actually doing was allowing himself to find imagery that expressed his emotions – had he not done this, then he might have fallen into a neurosis or even ultimately a full-blown psychosis.

Discovering archetypes

Jung found that as he wrote about his dreams and visions he was often using 'high-flown language'. He found this pomposity rather embarrassing, and often felt strong resistance to his fantasies, but he tried to treat the whole thing as a sort of scientific experiment. He knew all too well the dangers of becoming prey to his own fantasies, and how easy it would be to slide into psychosis. Frequently, he imagined himself going down a steep descent, until he reached levels as deep as 300 m. After that he felt himself in a cosmic abyss of empty space. He felt as if he was entering the land of the dead, and there he began to encounter strange beings.

In one vision he met two figures: a beautiful young girl, accompanied by an old man with a beard. These figures were examples of what Jung called archetypes – recurring images or patterns of thinking that represent a typical human experience. These form the basic content of religion, myth, art and legend. They are part of the collective unconscious and they emerge in the individual psyche through dreams and visions. Encounters with archetypal figures are often accompanied by a feeling of a numinous presence, and the language they use is often the 'high-flown' language that Jung referred to.

Jung felt that the old man in his vision corresponded to Elijah, an Old Testament prophet, and the young girl to Salome, the archetypal seductress found in the New Testament. He thought that they made a strange couple, but to his astonishment Elijah assured him that they had belonged together for all eternity. Years later, he came to realize that this odd couple indeed appeared frequently together in myths. Jung's Elijah character is the wise old prophet who represents intellect and knowledge, while Salome represents the erotic element. In Jung's vision they were also accompanied by a large black snake, which Jung explains is a frequent counterpart to the mythic hero.

After a while, Jung discovered another archetypal figure who seemed to evolve out of the Elijah figure. This was Philemon, a pagan sage with Gnostic ideas. He first appeared to Jung in a dream, as an old man flying out of a blue sky with clods of earth floating in it. He had the horns of a bull and the wings of a kingfisher. He carried a bunch of four keys, one of which he held as if ready to open a lock. Jung painted a picture of this apparition and, to his great astonishment, shortly afterwards found a newly dead kingfisher in his garden by the lakeshore. This was most odd, as kingfishers were rare in the area. Jung saw the incident as an example of the kind of meaningful coincidence that he called **synchronicity** (see Chapter 08). He said that coincidences of this sort provide a crucial insight that there are things in the psyche that we do not produce – they produce themselves and have their own life. He began to have lengthy conversations with Philemon and even went for walks with him in the garden. Philemon explained to Jung that we do not generate our own thoughts – they have an external reality of their own, just like birds in the air, or people in a room.

Our thoughts have an external reality of their own.

Jung commented that it was Philemon who taught him 'psychic objectivity, the reality of the psyche'. He realized that there was something within him that could talk about matters that he did not consciously know about, and which might even act against him. Archetypal encounters were very important because they enabled Jung to give a personal form to aspects of his unconscious. Because they were in some way 'separate' from himself, he was able to bring them into relationship with his conscious mind and not get too bogged down in some of their more disturbing utterances. Philemon became an important guru to Jung – psychologically he seemed to have superior insight. Years later, Jung met a very cultivated Indian who was a friend of Ghandi. He was pleased when he found that this man had no problem with the idea of a spirit guru, and indeed said that many people have them.

Another archetypal fantasy figure called Ka arose in Jung's mind. Ka seemed to come from deep in the earth. Jung painted a picture of him as a herm – a stone pillar with a head on top – with his upper part made of bronze. Philemon was a winged spirit and represented the spiritual aspect, whereas Ka was the spirit of nature, a kind of earth demon who could obscure the **halcyon** spirit of meaning, or replace it with beauty.

Jung saw it as ironic that he, a psychiatrist, was encountering the same kind of imagery in his own unconscious that he observed emerging from the minds of the insane. But he realized that the sea of unconscious imagery which confused his mental patients was also the matrix of the collective unconscious – the mythopoeic imagination. Eventually he was able to understand the archetypal figures of Philemon and Ka much better and integrate them through his study of alchemy.

In 1916, Jung decided that he wanted to give some kind of concrete form to the ideas and insights that had come from Philemon. A restless, ominous atmosphere was beginning to gather in his home. The children had started seeing white figures at night, and had even had their blankets snatched away from them in bed. The doorbell rang frantically when there was nobody there, and the whole house felt thick with spirits. Eventually, a whole host of spirits apparently infiltrated the house, saying to Jung, 'We have come back from Jerusalem where we found not what we sought.' At this point, Jung put pen to paper and started writing – the writing poured out of him for three days. He called this writing *Septem Sermones ad Mortuos* (*Seven Sermons to the Dead*). This is a long poetic piece, in a very archaic style, written as if the author were addressing the dead. It represented an exteriorization of all that had been going on in Jung's turbulent mind, and the spirits all vanished from the house as soon as he began to write it – the weird haunting was over.

Seven Sermons to the Dead was first published anonymously, and by his own request it was not included in the 20 volumes of Jung's collected works. However, he saw the work as a prelude to what he wanted to communicate to the world about the unconscious. It is a difficult piece to understand, but it contains outlines of some of his most important ideas, such as the endless battle between opposites in the psyche, and the concept of individuation. Many of the ideas in it are derived from Gnostic writing, for example it mentions a god called Abraxas, who is a solar deity with a cock's head. Abraxas combines good and evil in one form, an idea that Jung was to develop later in his thinking about the nature of God, when he wrote *Answer to Job*. In *Seven Sermons* he describes the Gnostic concept of the 'pleroma', which refers to God and everything that emanates from God. Because all things are contained in the pleroma, everything is balanced and therefore becomes void – a bit like the idea of matter and anti-matter cancelling one another out. However, in individual humans, although opposites are apparent, they are *not* balanced, and this is what gives us our individuality. Therefore, the task of the individual is to pursue his own distinctiveness in the long, soul-searching process of individuation.

Jung suggests that the spirits he encountered just before he wrote *Seven Sermons to the Dead* had in fact been **parapsychological** phenomena, somehow cause by his own highly charged emotional state. The fact that others in the household were clearly affected as well seems to support Jung's idea that psychic activity, and indeed the archetypes themselves, can extend beyond the mind of the individual. In *The Structure and Dynamics of the Psyche* (see *Collected Works*, Volume 8 in **Further reading**) he gives an example of archetypal imagery appearing in the hallucinations of one of his patients. The man in question was in his thirties and suffered form a paranoid form of schizophrenia, which meant that he presented a strange mixture of normal intelligence, fantastic ideas and hallucinations. During his quieter phases he was allowed to wander around the hospital corridors, and it was there that Jung found him one day, gazing at the sun out of a window. He explained to Jung that if one looked at the sun with eyes half shut, one could see the sun's phallus. If one moved one's head the sun-phallus would move too, and that was the origin of the wind. This notion seems totally crazy, but four years later Jung read about a Greek papyrus that had only recently been translated which gave an account of a vision where exactly the same phenomenon was described – a kind of tube, hanging from the disc of the sun, which is the 'origin of the ministering wind'. The patient who had told him about the sun-phallus had been committed to the mental hospital before this translation was available – this was important for Jung because he realized that it could not be a case of **cryptomnesia** (from the Greek 'hidden memory'), where an experience is forgotten before being later reproduced without the person recognizing it as a memory. He gradually found other references in art and mythology to a similar idea – that of the wind, or the divine spirit, emanating from the disc of the sun. Jung was fascinated by exploring archetypal thinking of this sort, and many other examples appear throughout his writing.

Mandalas

As mentioned in Chapter 01, towards the end of the First World War, Jung began to emerge from his period of great darkness. While he was stationed at Château d'Oex in 1918–19, he began to draw and experiment with 'mandala' drawings. The word 'mandala' comes from Sanskrit and means a 'magic circle'. A basic mandala is usually a circle containing a square or occasionally some other symmetrical figure, but there are many variations. There is usually some kind of symbolic imagery, most commonly a cross, flower or wheel, usually with four as the basis of the structure. They are found in many cultures and contexts, for example they frequently appear in Yogic tradition, where they are used symbolically to depict the chakras, or energy centres of the body. They are also common in Christian art of the early Middle Ages. Even the earlier Celtic cross could be seen as a simple mandala.

Jung had produced his first mandala painting in 1916, after writing *Seven Sermons,* but he had not understood it properly at the time. Now he began to sketch small circular drawings of this type every morning in his notebook. He observed the ways in which they changed from day to day and found that they helped him to chart his own psychic development – the ever-changing state of his inner self. He realized that the image of the mandala may represent the universe itself, or the 'inner universe' – the wholeness of what he referred to as the **Self** (this is often spelt with a capital S to distinguish it from everyday usage of the same word). The Self is the central archetype and it is the archetype of wholeness and order which transcends the ego.

Jung used the mandala to explore his ever-changing inner self.

Mandalas fascinated Jung for many years and he gradually came to understand that they represent the way in which all paths in the psyche lead eventually to a mid-point, the centre of the mandala, which is the core or essence of the Self. The goal of psychic development is the discovery of this unique Self. This process is what Jung called 'individuation': the conscious realisation and fulfilment of a person's unique being. It is one of the core concepts of analytical psychology. Jung explained that the evolution of the psyche is not linear, but a process of 'circumambulation (walking around) of the self'.

Jung found that mandalas tended to appear when the psyche was in a state of turmoil and disorientation. The archetype that appears on the mandala represents a pattern of order and balancing. He compared this to a psychological 'viewfinder', marked with a cross or circle divided into four. This is superimposed on the psychic chaos, so that everything falls into its correct place and is held together by the outer circle. Jung found that his own mandala drawings linked up with external experiences in his everyday life and also with his dreams. For example, he did two mandalas that seemed to be related to one another. The first was inspired by a dream where he was in Liverpool amid rain and fog. Suddenly he came upon an island with a magnolia tree in full blossom upon it. This dream felt very important – Liverpool was the 'pool of life'. When he painted this mandala he felt it was in some way Chinese. Later he did another mandala with a golden castle at the centre of it.

Soon after this, Jung received a letter containing a manuscript of 1,000-year-old Taoist alchemical writing from China. It was called *The Secret of the Golden Flower*. He related the symbol of the golden flower to the golden castle he had drawn and the beautiful magnolia tree he had dreamed of. In both cases the circular pattern with the goal in the centre somehow expressed for him the totality of the individual, in both conscious and unconscious aspects. In Eastern religions the mandala is often used in a similar way, as a centring device to help with meditation exercises. From Jung's mandala work emerged inklings of his own personal myth, his all-important 'story' that expressed his real being.

The tower at Bollingen

Jung felt that he was able gradually to put his dreams and fantasies onto a more solid footing and begin to understand the unconscious in more scientific terms. He also wanted to make a representation of his innermost thoughts and knowledge in a more permanent, solid way than simply writing them down on paper. In 1922, he bought some land at Bollingen, near the shore of the upper lake of Zürich, about 40 km away from the family home at Küsnacht. To fulfill this yearning for self-expression, and also as a quiet retreat, he began to construct a second home here. At first he had the idea of a simple round structure with a hearth in the centre, like a primitive dwelling hut. This arrangement would give a feeling of simplicity and wholeness, with the life of the family centring around the hearth. However, as he began to build, Jung realized that this was too simple, and the structure gradually evolved into a medieval-looking building complete with a tower.

Jung kept on adding to this building throughout his long life, the new bits all representing different parts of his ever-evolving psyche. He felt that this was an important part of his own individuation process, as if he was being reborn in stone. From the beginning he saw the tower as a place symbolising maturation, a 'maternal womb' in which he could express his developing being. Everything there was connected to him and he himself was inextricably linked with the surrounding landscape. There is an inscription above the original entrance which reads, 'Sanctuary of Philemon, penitence of Faust'. The reference to Faust is connected to Goethe's story *Faust,* about a philosopher who encounters his own demonic shadow side.

Life at Bollingen was kept deliberately simple – there was no electricity, and Jung chopped all his own wood, drew water from a well and cooked all his own food. He remarked that these simple acts made him feel simple himself – something which is difficult for man to achieve. He enjoyed the sense of silence in the place and living in harmony with nature. This allowed thoughts from long ago to rise to the surface. The land upon which the tower was built was steeped in history, having formerly belonged to the monastery of St Gall; Jung also felt a sense of time stretching ahead into a remote future, so that he saw life 'in the round' as a continuous flow.

Jung made a special resting room within the tower where no one but he was allowed to go without permission. Here he did paintings on the walls and found that he could truly be himself. He found a great sense of inner peace and spiritual concentration when he visited the tower. Whenever he was there he felt most deeply himself, able to relax into personality

Number 2, the creative part of himself which existed outside the confines of time. All around the tower he carved stones, with inscriptions expressing different insights. One of these, carved in 1950, bears various images and inscriptions, including lines quoted from a Latin verse by alchemist Arnaldus Villanova (died 1913):

Here stands the mean uncomely stone,
'tis very cheap in price!
The more it is despised by fools,
the more loved by the wise.

The verse refers to the alchemist's stone, the 'Lapis Philosophorum', which represents spiritual insight that is not understood by most people and hence is despised and rejected. Jung said that this stone was like an explanation of the meaning of the tower and its occupant, which reminded him of the legend of Merlin's life in the forest after he had vanished from the world. Men still heard his cries, but nobody could understand or interpret them.

The creative play aspect that Jung enjoyed at Bollingen was very important for him as a means for accessing his unconscious. He found that most people found it very difficult to explore and understand their own unconscious, but emphasized that only through doing so can we become whole.

Summary

- Jung had a midlife crisis that he used in a constructive way to explore his own psyche and develop his ideas about the ways in which the psyche operates.
- Myths were very important to Jung because he saw them as expressions of ideas from the collective unconscious.
- Through listening to his inner thoughts and feelings, Jung discovered the importance of creative play as a way of unlocking the unconscious. He himself used this technique throughout his life whenever he needed to relax or find inspiration.
- He also worked with dreams, visions and fantasies, both his own and those of his patients, finding that these often gave insight into the person's inner world.

- Archetypal encounters were important to Jung because they helped him to personify aspects of his unconscious and so bring them into relationship with his conscious mind.
- The real goal of psychic development is individuation – the discovery of the true Self. Jung found that the mandala was an excellent symbol of this process and a useful way of mapping progress.

04

exploring the psyche

In this chapter you will learn:
- Jung's theories about the structure and dynamics of the psyche
- the part played by the personal and the collective unconscious
- how balancing pairs of opposites operate in the psyche.

The structure of the psyche

Jung's ideas about the psyche are not always easy to grasp and people are still disagreeing about exactly what he meant by concepts such as archetypes. This is partly because he was trying to formulate scientific theories about abstract concepts. When he talks about the psyche Jung means the whole of the mind or spirit, both conscious and unconscious. He uses the words 'psyche' and 'psychic', rather than 'mind' and 'mental', because the latter usually refer only to a conscious state. He talks about the psyche more as if it were a process than a thing. The individual psyche is always changing as it seeks growth and wholeness, and should not to be confused with the Self, which is the goal that the psyche is constantly seeking and moving towards. Conscious attitudes within the psyche are always balanced by unconscious attitudes – if a conscious attitude grows too strong then the unconscious will always seek to restore equilibrium. The unconscious will express its ideas by means of dreams, fantasies, spontaneous imagery, slips of the tongue and so on. If the unconscious message is ignored then neurosis or even physical disease may result.

In order to understand Jung's ideas about the structure of the psyche it will help first to look at what Freud had said, because his ideas reflected the cutting-edge thinking of the times. In accordance with his insistence upon scientific thinking, Freud grappled with trying to formulate a theory about the structure of the psyche. This was obviously difficult to achieve – one cannot capture the psyche under a microscope or measure it in the laboratory. One of the main difficulties was that, although Freud believed that the brain was the organ that controlled human consciousness, he realized, as Jung did later, that the 'divisions' of the psyche he described could not be physical divisions of this organ. They really just provided a descriptive model to try and help us towards a better understanding of what was going on in the psyche.

To begin with Freud decided that there were two states of consciousness:

- **The conscious mind** is the part of the mind that is aware of its own thoughts and actions. This is where all conscious thought processes occur – it is the source of conscious thinking, ideas and understanding. It is concerned with logical thinking, reality and civilized behaviour.
- **The unconscious** is seen by Freud as the part of the mind that is repressed, the place where we put all the ideas and thoughts

that our conditioning does not allow us to look at. Information in the unconscious cannot easily be accessed. Much of our past history lies here too, some of which can only be recalled under hypnosis.

After a while, Freud decided that this simple division was not quite right, so he proposed the existence of a third level:

- **The preconscious** is the region of the mind between the conscious and the unconscious, where information is stored that is not conscious at the moment, but can easily be recalled when needed.

Like Freud, Jung suggests that the psyche has three main levels, but his interpretation differs from Freud's:

- **The conscious mind** – Jung's concept here is similar to Freud's. Jung pointed out that our immediate consciousness is personal to the individual and is the only part of the psyche that we can really study experimentally. The ego is the centre of consciousness and the sense of identity. It organizes perception, memory, thoughts and feelings. Everything else within the psyche is unconscious, and can only be accessed indirectly. This can happen by means of dream analysis, creative play and so on.
- **The personal unconscious** – this area of the psyche is unique to the individual. It is formed from repressed wishes and impulses, subliminal perceptions and forgotten experiences. Psychic contents that the ego does not recognize, or are not immediately accessible to it, are found in this area. It has two main types of contents:
  a) Contents that have become unconscious either because they simply lost their intensity and were forgotten, or because they have been repressed – that is, consciousness has been actively withdrawn from them. This includes traumatic memories and material which threatens the ego.
  b) Contents that have entered the psyche but have never had sufficient intensity to reach consciousness. This category would include many of the sense impressions that we are constantly bombarded with, because we cannot possibly pay conscious attention to them all.
- **The collective unconscious** – this is made up of archetypes and is not individual, but rather is common to all people. It cannot be built up like the personal unconscious, because it is already fully formed within the individual. Jung saw the collective unconscious as the true basis of the individual psyche.

Jung viewed the human psyche with reverential awe, saying that it had a transcendent dimension and was part of the 'inmost mystery of life'. He strongly disagreed with the mechanistic view, which tended to regard the psyche as a side-effect of physical and chemical processes. He did not see how one could reduce the psyche to something measurable in a laboratory – after all, how could a mere 'secretion of the brain' observe itself and grapple with the nature of the universe? In common with Eastern and shamanic philosophy, Jung did not see any validity in separating 'material reality' from the whole of existence. He did not view the body and the psyche as separate entities either, but as part of one and the same being. He recognized that if the psyche is malfunctioning it can harm the body, just as, conversely, a physical illness can adversely affect the psyche. Modern medical science has only recently begun to catch up with Jung's thinking and view human beings in a more holistic way. Jung maintained that every science is a function of the psyche and so all knowledge is rooted in it: the psyche, he said, is the 'greatest of all cosmic wonders'. You can read more about Jung's views on the structure of the psyche and the way it works in *The Structure and Dynamics of the Psyche*, Volume 8 of his collected works.

The personal unconscious

The concept of people having an unconscious mind that can affect the way they behave was not new when Jung was formulating his theories. In fact, people had been aware of the idea for centuries, but Freud was the first to pull different ideas together and make the unconscious a subject for serious scientific study. Before Freud, the unconscious had been largely overlooked or even ignored altogether by the scientific community. Freud's work had made people much more aware of the unconscious and the ways in which it operated in both the adult and the developing child. He believed that accessing unconscious repressed memories connected with childhood sexual trauma was the key to combatting neuroses.

Freud was a convinced mechanist and tried always to be strictly scientific in his approach. Jung was also trained in the scientific method and tried to understand the workings of the psyche in terms of biological processes. However, unlike many scientists of his day, Jung never lost his interest in the psychic and paranormal aspects of the human mind. He acknowledged that there was much in life that we cannot yet understand, but this did not mean that one had to pretend it did not exist. In a lecture to the Society for Psychical Research in 1919, he expressed this point of view when he remarked, 'I shall not commit the fashionable stupidity of regarding everything I cannot explain as a fraud.' This difference in attitude was one of several key factors in the rift between Freud and Jung.

Freud's hostile attitude towards the paranormal irritated Jung, because he saw it as narrow and limiting in its understanding of the psyche. His own aim was to study the many and varied aspects of both the personal unconscious and the collective unconscious, even though he recognized that this was an enormous task. One night when he was visiting Freud, he asked him what he thought about **precognition** and parapsychology in general. Freud's reply was terse and dismissive and Jung felt that he had to bite his tongue to conceal his irritation. As he did so he felt his diaphragm grow very hot, and then there was a loud bang in Freud's bookcase right next to them, so that both men jumped up in alarm. Jung announced that this was an example of 'catalytic exteriorization phenomenon' (what we would now probably call psychokinesis). Freud scoffed at this idea, saying that it was 'sheer bosh', but Jung contradicted him and predicted a second loud bang to prove his point. This immediately happened, no doubt leaving Jung feeling smug and Freud aghast!

Like Freud, Jung was convinced that the unconscious had enormous influence, but Jung viewed the unconscious in a totally different way. Freud's influence in current thinking had turned the unconscious into a sort of mental rubbish heap, a 'dump for moral refuse'. For Jung, though, the unconscious was much more than that – it contained *all* aspects of human nature, 'light and dark, beautiful and ugly, good and evil, profound and silly'. Jung saw this balancing of opposites as basic to the structure of the psyche.

Complexes

In Jung's view the personal unconscious consists mainly of **complexes**. These are related groups of emotionally charged ideas, thoughts and images. Many complexes may appear in the same person, but they do not have to be negative in effect. They are psychic phenomena that tend to group together because they work more efficiently that way. This is because they tend to be related to a particular archetype. A commonly cited example is the 'mother complex'. There is an inbuilt instinctual ability to recognize the mother's nipple and this is our first experience of 'mother'. Gradually, we add to this all kinds of information about our own mother, and mothers in general, and build up an inner data bank – this is the mother complex. This is constantly expanding and changing as a person matures, so that we may add to it a whole host of other ideas, such as 'mother earth', 'mother nature', 'mother country' and so on. All these relate to the mother archetype and help the psyche to be more organized and efficient.

Complexes can act as a kind of sub-personality, and at times these can manifest themselves as a different character. Such a character may appear in dreams, fantasies or trance states. Jung first became aware of this phenomenon when his cousin Hélène Preiswerk manisfested the character of Ivenes in her mediumistic trance state. In cases of mental illness or neurosis, complexes may be in conflict with one another, or their energy may become blocked off. The more negatively charged complexes a person has the more disturbed he or she becomes, because these act as pathological, disrupting factors in the psyche. The immediate goal of analysis of the unconscious is to root out these negative complexes so that their content becomes conscious and the person can stop 'acting out' from them and being ruled by them. The unconscious is always in danger of becoming too one-sided, keeping to well worn paths and getting stuck in dead ends. We are all familiar with the idea of somebody having 'a one-track mind'. Jung stressed that we are never done with working on the unconscious, and should always pay attention to our dreams and fantasies, because they will give us pointers as to where we have become unbalanced.

The collective unconscious

Jung made a great discovery that led him to a whole new approach to psychology. He said that, 'just as conscious contents can vanish into the unconscious, new contents, which have never yet been conscious, can *arise* from it.' In other words, the unconscious was no mere rubbish dump, as Freud had maintained, but was infinitely mysterious and full of the seeds of future events and ideas, as well as those from the past. Not only could it look forward as well as back in time, it could also reach beyond its individual boundaries into the world of the collective unconscious.

The collective unconscious is different from the personal unconscious because it does not evolve out of personal experience and is therefore not a personal acquisition, unique to the individual. The personal unconscious is composed mainly of contents that have at some time been in consciousness, and have then been forgotten or repressed. The contents of the collective unconscious, on the other hand, have never been conscious and they are not acquired, but inherited. The collective unconscious has two main aspects:

- **archetypes** – the psychic patterns that help to give form to our understanding of unconscious ideas;
- **instincts** – the innate biological drives that determine our behaviour. Examples are the sex drive, hunger and aggression.

Both these components belong in the collective unconscious because they exist independently of the individual psyche and contain universally recognized, inherited aspects.

Archetypes

The word archetype is derived from the Greek words *arche* meaning 'first' and *type* meaning 'imprint' or 'pattern'. Archetypes are seen as being like deposits of experiences that have been frequently repeated in the history of mankind. These patterns are present in all humans from birth, and reside as energy at a deep level of the unconscious. They can be encountered inwardly in dreams and fantasy, or externally in myths and religious teaching. An archetype can be experienced in many ways – as a story; as a pattern or an image, such as a mandala; as a mythical or archetypal character; or even as an emotional feeling.

To explain better how archetypes operate, Jung gives the example of the universally observable phenomenon of the daily journey of the sun across the sky. This gave rise to the myth of the sun-hero, who typically dies and is reborn in an endless cycle. Variations on this theme are fundamental to many religions. In this way a natural, physical process gives rise to a subjective fantasy, which is then incorporated into a universally recognizable myth. Jung says that archetypes are usually religious in their nature, and are accompanied by an atmosphere of the numinous when they appear in our dreams and fantasies, impelling us to behave in ways that re-enact the original process.

Archetypes are patterns or images and have no physical existence in the material world, but Jung emphasizes that this does not mean that they have no separate reality of their own. Of course, this makes them hard to envisage as biological entities, and Jung was inclined later in life to steer away from the strictly biological aspects of his psychology. On the other hand, he says that the problem of whether the archetypes ever 'originated' at all is a metaphysical question and therefore unanswerable. He was more interested in exploring how archetypes actually worked, and how they affected human behaviour, rather than in attempting to explain their origins. A good example of the way Jung understood archetypes is shown in his spirit guide Philemon, who is an archetypal sage or wise man, who seemed to have a 'separate' identity of his own. In fantasies like this the archetype is manifesting as an image, which helps us to understand deeply unconscious ideas by making them into something we can grasp – a bit like drawing a picture of something in order to explain how it works.

People will form different archetypal images according to the culture in which they live, but the archetype itself remains the same. Everyone is familiar with archetypal figures that appear in myths and fairy stories. Other examples are the old woman, the trickster, the youth, the fool, the 'baddie', and so on. Archetypes have both positive and negative aspects, which reflect the wholeness and balance of the psyche. For example, the mother archetype is reflected in the many different faces of the mother goddess, which include a nurturing goddess of grain and harvest, and a wild boar who devours her own offspring.

Jung was anxious to point out that he had not totally invented the idea of archetypes – they are often described as appearing in myths as 'motifs', and they also appear in other guises in anthropology and comparative religion, for example as 'primordial thoughts', or 'categories of the imagination'. Jung said that in order to understand the meaning of contents of the deep levels of the psyche we need mythology, because all myths are a sort of **projection** from the collective unconscious. This is a bit like using analytical techniques to understand the real meaning of a dream. He gives as an example the way people form constellations from the chaos of the stars in the night sky. These are then given numinous significance in the form of heroic and mythical figures and give rise to the idea of the influence of the stars as asserted by astrologers. What is really at work is the unconscious, introspective activity of the collective unconscious.

In a similar way, archetypal figures are projected in myths and legends, and also onto real historical figures. A good example is that of the King Arthur legends, where a man who was probably a real-life British chieftain has been enormously magnified into a mythical hero.

Instincts

Instincts are unconscious impulses or actions, and like archetypes they are inherited and collective. They compel us to act in specific, biologically determined ways. Whereas archetypes affect the ways in which we perceive and understand the world, instincts affect our behaviour. They exist in animals and birds and as well as humans. Like the archetypes, instincts are very ancient parts of the psyche, and as such they are very conservative in their form and functioning. Jung says that they appear in the mind as images, which express their impulses visually. He gives the example of the yucca moth, which has a symbiotic relationship with the plant of the same name. If we could explore this moth's psyche we would find a pattern of ideas that compel it to seek out and recognize a yucca plant.

Jung reflected that civilization has forced us to separate from our basic instincts, but they have not disappeared altogether. We still have instinctual drives towards finding food, having sex and so on. But these are often repressed because, in order to live in society, we have to learn that it is not always appropriate to act instinctually. This means that instincts tend to show themselves indirectly, for example as neurosis, or as unaccountable moods. They may also appear in dream images, or manifest as slips of the tongue or memory lapses.

Jung says that the unconscious is dominated by two fundamental instincts – the sexuality drive and the power drive. These two basic drives clash with one another, because the sexuality drive is basically to do with the preservation of the species, whereas the power drive is to do with the preservation of the individual. This is why society needs moral rules, in order to avoid the ensuing conflicts as much as possible.

However, Jung wanted to move away from the idea of separate instincts such as hunger, sex and aggression. He found this approach too concrete and decided that it was more helpful to see the various instincts as being different expressions of a single psychic energy. He called this motivating psychic energy 'libido', from the Latin word for desire or urge. He compared the concept with the one in physics, where heat, light and electricity are all different aspects of physical energy. Freud had used the term 'libido' to describe the sexual drive, claiming that it was the main motivating drive in the psyche, but Jung stressed that it is important not to pick on one single motivating instinct in this way, any more than the physicist would say that all forces derive from, say, heat alone.

For Jung the psyche is a dynamic system, constantly changing and self-regulating. Libido flows between two opposing poles, which Jung calls 'the opposites'. There are many opposites in the psyche, for example conscious/unconscious; sleeping/ waking; thinking/feeling; anger/peace. The greater the tension between two opposites, the greater the libido. The opposites have a regulating function in the psyche: when an extreme is reached the tendency is for libido to flow to the opposite state, so that, for example, rage becomes calm or love becomes hate.

Jung also says that there are two basic movements within the psyche. Forwards movement is called 'progression' and is concerned with adaptation to the environment. This echoes Jung's Number 1 personality, which was concerned with getting on in the world. The opposite state is backward movement, which is called 'regression'. This is concerned with the inner needs of the individual, and so we can relate this Jung's Number 2 personality, which was concerned with play and the inner world of dreams and fantasies. Both states are necessary in a balanced psyche. If natural balance is not found then libido tends to flow into the unconscious, where it will build up until it is expressed through some outlet such as fantasy, rage or even, in extreme cases, psychosis. Perhaps this is one reason why our modern society feels so unbalanced – we are all so busy working and progressing that we have no time for rest and restoration, play and dreams.

The ego and the Self

The ego (from the Latin word for 'I') is the centre of consciousness and gives us our sense of identity. Freud had been the first to use this term, but Jung developed the idea and came to understand it in a rather different way. Freud said that the main task of the ego was to tell us what is 'real' and to protect the psyche, maximising pleasure and minimizing pain. Jung, on the other hand, emphasizes the ego's role in helping us to function effectively in society. He does not really distinguish between ego and consciousness – in fact, he has a tendency to use the two words interchangeably, and sometimes combines them into one word, 'ego-consciousness'. The ego organizes and balances the conscious and unconscious aspects of the psyche, giving it a sense of personal identity and purpose. Jung came to identify his own ego with his analytical Number 1 personality.

Jung stresses that the ego is not the same as the Self, which is the whole personality and includes both conscious and unconscious aspects of the psyche. Like the unconscious, the Self already exists when we are born, and the ego emerges out of it in the course of childhood development. It seeks biological goals, but is also interested in the spiritual and the numinous because it has a transcendent quality. The overall goal of the Self is to make the individual complete and whole. It is often depicted symbolically in images such as mandalas. The health of the ego depends upon the health of the Self.

We need to develop a strong and effective ego in order to function in the outer world. This is the chief task that we have to accomplish in the first half of life, as we learn to grow away from our parents and do things for ourselves. A strong ego can exert a balancing influence, keeping the conscious and unconscious aspects of the personality in equilibrium. An over-inflated ego, on the other hand, will form a dictatorial, intolerant personality. Such an ego can become highly unpleasant, even dangerous, seeing itself as all-important, almost god-like.

During the second half of life the ego and the Self begin to confront one another and gradually we begin to understand that the Self is actually more important. At this stage, the personality can begin to integrate and eventually we may attain higher consciousness. Evidently most people never reach this stage in the individuation process!

The shadow and projection

The shadow

The **shadow** is an unconscious part of the personality that contains weaknesses and other aspects of personality that a person cannot admit to having. Everyone has a shadow, and the less consciously we are aware of it, the blacker and denser it is, because psychic contents that we repress can never be corrected.

The ego and the shadow work together as a balancing pair. Jung related the shadow to his intuitive Number 2 personality. It is usually the first hidden layer of the personality to be encountered when a person begins psychological analysis. One of the primary tasks of the analyst is to begin to make a person aware of the relationship between the ego and the shadow. When a person has a very weak ego they may be in danger of becoming swamped by images from the shadow, rather as Jung himself was during his midlife crisis.

The shadow is the dark side of our nature – all that we see as being inferior or uncivilized. It often appears in dreams as a dark, usually rather negative figure, who is always the same sex as the dreamer. In waking life it is particularly in interactions with people of the same sex that our shadow self is revealed. In same-sex groups we tend to do things that we would not even think of doing when we are on our own. The reason we do this is often to be part of the group and not to appear foolish – rather as Jung discovered himself behaving when he was at school.

The ego wishes to hide shadow aspects of the personality, but in fact the shadow is not necessarily bad, so much as primitive in its outlook. If we face our shadow properly then it can offer us integration between the conscious and unconscious parts of our psyche. By seeing our own shadow we also see our own light. Once we can look at and understand these two opposites within us we can find the middle ground.

Projection

An over-inflated ego often projects the shadow onto other people. Projection is a process where an unconscious characteristic, a fault, or even a talent of one's own is seen as belonging to another person or object. It is a normal and natural process and can be positive or negative in character. It is always accompanied by a strong emotional reaction to a person, object or situation. Obvious examples are falling in love (this is projection of the **anima** or **animus**, which is the opposite-sex aspect of the psyche, explored later in this chapter), or taking an excessive dislike to someone or something. Projection is an indication that unconscious ideas are trying to break through into the conscious mind. It is not really the other person or thing that we love or loathe, but a part of our own psyche that is projected onto them. It is important here to distinguish between the idea of 'falling in love', which is like having a crush on someone, and the more stable type of love that develops with maturity.

A good example of projection, which also shows how it inevitably tends to break down eventually, is Jung's 'crush' on Freud. We could say that Jung was projecting a 'father archetype' onto Freud. Whenever projection like this occurs it is very difficult to behave rationally and objectively, so the situation tends to lead to conflict. Jung found that, on the one hand he tended to hang upon Freud's every word, seeing him as a sort of guru; on the other hand he felt a nagging resistance to his teachings and gradually became highly critical of him. This divided attitude shows that he was still unaware of the underlying subconscious issues that were involved in the relationship. As the psyche matures it is often able to recognize and own its shadow characteristics and the projection is then withdrawn. When we project we tend to drink in all the attitudes of the other person, and repress criticisms that are trying to surface from our own psyche. These criticisms often appear in dreams – outwardly, Jung thought of Freud as wise and experienced, but in one of his dreams he saw him as a peevish and petty royal official!

When the shadow is projected, the ego sees the other person or people as being evil and can conveniently deny any nasty aspects of itself. In order for true integration to occur within the psyche, it is necessary for us to accept our shadow and find ways in which the conscious personality and the shadow can live together. If we are brave enough to withdraw our shadow projections, then we become aware of our own shadow. This is difficult for us, and represents a huge moral task, because we are no longer able to blame others for our problems. We then become aware that whatever is wrong in the world 'out there' is also wrong with ourselves – the dark aspects of our own psyche become present and real. Jung says that if we can learn to deal with our own shadow then we have done something very real for the world, shouldering our own tiny part of the gigantic burden of unsolved social problems.

Jung stresses that the psyche is not confined to the individual. Groups have a collective psyche that forms the spirit of the age, or Zeitgeist. This collective psyche readily forms a collective shadow, which can be exceedingly dangerous. For example, in the Second World War, the Nazis formed a collective shadow which they projected onto the Jewish people, whom they then saw as being worthless and evil.

Jung urged mankind to take a good look at itself. He sensed dark uncontrolled shadow forces building up in civilized society. Society has a tendency to keep its problem aspects tucked away in separate drawers, and as a result these deadly, self-created dangers are often projected onto other nations. Jung gave as an example the perceived threat by the Western nations from the communist countries behind the Iron Curtain. He said that we must recognize that shadow projections are moral problems, which cannot be solved by arms races or economic competition. We need to look at our own shadow, instead of blaming 'them' all the time. Unfortunately, we have yet to learn this lesson.

The persona

The **persona** (from the same Latin word, meaning an 'actor's mask') is like a mask that the ego creates in order to hide its true nature from society. It is our public face and may be assumed both deliberately and unconsciously. Whenever we relate to others we put on this mask, which has a dual function – to make an impression upon others and to conceal what we feel to be our true nature. The form of the mask depends upon the expectations and conditioning of society from parents, teachers, peer groups and so on.

Hiding behind the persona.

It is necessary for each individual sometimes to assume a persona in order to function normally within society, because it gives some degree of protection to the vulnerable ego. We need it in order to be able to fit in with a certain culture, or to do a particular job for example. Problems only arise when a person totally identifies with the persona, which means that the person becomes nothing but the role they play. Behaviour becomes very rigid, and the person is fearful of ever dropping the mask. Such a personality becomes very confined and liable to develop neuroses. There is a failure to see the broader aspects of life beyond the ego's own tiny role, and this situation is spiritually suffocating.

Every profession has its own persona, and it is quite easy for people to become totally identified with their professional image and hide behind it all the time. Jung went so far as to say that the persona is in fact a kind of false personality that an individual may ultimately end up believing is real. In his quietly humorous way, Jung describes meeting a very venerable man, whom one could almost describe as a saint. For three days Jung's feeling of inadequacy and inferiority in the face of this person built up and he was beginning seriously to consider how he could improve himself. Then the man's wife came to him for analysis. This was a real revelation, as Jung realized that a man who becomes one with his persona can cheerfully project all his shortcomings onto his wife without her noticing – but she pays the price by developing a serious neurosis!

Anima and animus

The outer personality and attitude is what Jung calls the persona, but he believed that everyone also has an inner personality and attitude, which is turned towards the world of the unconscious. Jung used the word 'anima' to describe the personification of the unconscious feminine aspect of a man's personality. The 'animus' is the corresponding masculine aspect of a woman's personality. These unconscious aspects of the personality are seen as being very important in regulating behaviour. Their character is complementary to the character of the persona, so that they commonly contain all the human qualities that are absent from the persona. Jung gives the example of the aggressive tyrant who is tormented by inner fear and bad dreams, or the intellectual man who is inwardly sentimental.

The anima

The anima is usually personified by the unconscious as a female figure. This figure – referred to by Jung as a 'soul-image' – will appear in dreams as an archetypal figure, such as the seductress, harlot or divine female spirit guide. She represents a man's feeling nature, which is fascinating and secretive. Because the anima is composed of feelings, she may distort a man's understanding, which Jung assumes to be based on logic. She is often associated with earth and water imagery, such as caves, fertile soil, waterfalls or the sea.

Jung first became aware of his own anima when he was analysing his fantasies during his midlife crisis. He asked himself what he was actually doing, and was startled to hear a woman's voice quite clearly announcing, 'it is art'. He felt cross about this and replied that it was nothing to do with art, but the voice again insisted that it was. This voice was the voice of his anima. At first he found her to be a negative force and felt somewhat in awe of her, but he carefully wrote down all their conversations.

Jung soon realized that by personifying an archetype in this way he was able to bring it into relationship with his own consciousness. This helps to make the archetype less powerful. Jung found his own anima to be 'full of deep cunning'. He saw her as being like everything that is 'unconscious, dark, equivocal and purposeless in a woman', and also mentioned 'her vanity, frigidity, helplessness and so forth'. He realized that if he had taken what she said at face value then he would have seen his work as being rather unreal, like watching a film, so that he would have felt detached from it. He seemed quite afraid of the potential power of the anima, saying that this kind of thinking could 'utterly destroy a man'.

Jung also recognized the more positive aspects of the anima, seeing that it is she who communicates the images of the unconscious to a man's conscious mind. Jung always questioned his own anima when he felt emotionally disturbed. He found that after a while she would always produce a useful image of some sort and his sense of unrest would vanish. For a man to be in touch with his anima is therefore healing and balancing. The anima is not a specific woman – her archetype contains all the ancestral impressions of what it means to be female. Her personified form in the individual psyche will depend very much upon a man's personal knowledge of women, which is rooted in his relationship with his mother, plus impressions gained about other women as he is growing up. Passionate attractions occur when the anima is projected onto an actual woman, so that the man falls in love. If, on the other hand, the man over-identifies with the anima, he may become moody, resentful or effeminate. If a man's anima is very weak then he will find relationships with women difficult.

The animus

Jung does not say as much about the corresponding animus in women, probably because he had no direct experience of it in his own psyche and this limited his understanding. Emma Jung explored the idea of the animus further and you can read about this in two essays in *Animus and Anima* (see **Further reading**). The animus represents the thinking, logical part of the woman's psyche and he can lead her towards knowledge and true meaning. It is made up of spontaneous, unpremeditated opinions that can affect a woman's emotional life. The animus appears in dreams as heroes, poets, gurus and judges. He is also represented in imagery of the air and fire elements, such as swords or burning flames. The animus projects onto sporting heroes, intellectuals and so on. Projection of the animus onto a real man results in the woman falling in love.

Projection of the animus results in a woman falling in love.

If a woman over-identifies with the animus, she becomes dominating, opinionated and stubborn. The woman's animus development is important in the way she relates to men – if it is weak, then she will have problems.

Ideas about the archetypal male or female from myths, dreams and fantasies can lead people to have very distorted ideas about the opposite sex. For example, the little girl who has been raised on Sleeping Beauty type stories might constantly seek a handsome prince. Jung believed that men are naturally polygamous, and that the anima compensates for this by always appearing as a single woman or female image. Women, on the other hand, are naturally monogamous, so the animus may compensate by appearing as whole groups of men.

If they function properly, both anima and animus should act like a sort of bridge or door between the personal unconscious and the collective unconscious. For this reason it is useful to get in touch with our anima or animus, because they have valuable messages for us. They also have a huge role to play in making relationships with the opposite sex successful. Together they form a 'syzygy' (from the same Greek word meaning 'yoked together'). We are always looking for our 'other half' – the half that we feel is missing – in members of the opposite sex. This is another good example of Jung's idea about the balanced opposites that are so basic to the functioning of the psyche.

Summary

- Jung emphasized that it is important to study both the personal unconscious and collective unconscious if we are to understand the human psyche.
- Archetypes are helpful because they give form to ideas from the collective unconscious.
- Jung did not find it helpful to identify separate driving instincts within the psyche, preferring instead to use the term libido to describe a general psychic energy.
- The ego (who we think we are) and the shadow (negative aspects of ourselves that we deny) work together in the psyche as a balancing pair.
- The persona is the mask that we wear in order to relate to other people.
- The male psyche has a balancing female aspect (the anima), and the female psyche has a corresponding male aspect (the animus).
- Projection occurs when we see an unconscious characteristic of our own in another person or object.

05

the journey of the psyche

In this chapter you will learn:

- the nature of the psyche's journey through life
- in more depth about individuation and the Self
- key features of the stages of development through which the psyche passes.

The journey of the psyche

In the previous chapter we looked at the way the psyche is constructed. This chapter will explore the ways in which it develops and operates. Jung suggested several basic principles at work, all of which he based on scientific principles:

- **The principle of opposites.** Everything in the psyche naturally has an opposite aspect, and in fact this principle is basic to all of nature. Think of up/down, light/dark and so on. Following this principle, every 'good' content in the psyche tends to be balanced by an equivalent 'bad' content. The flow of libido (psychic energy) between opposites is greater when there is a greater contrast between the opposites. This flow of libido drives our behaviour.

- **The principle of equivalence.** Equal amounts of energy are given to each of the opposites. If we deny the energy that is trying to flow towards negative aspects of the psyche, then we will tend to develop negative complexes as the energy is blocked up. These will emerge from the unconscious in dreams and fantasies, slips of tongue and so on.

- **The principle of entropy.** This is borrowed from physics and describes the tendency for all systems to 'run down' as energy is evenly distributed. In the psyche this means that opposites tend eventually to blend together – we can see this, for example, in the way people tend often to 'mellow' as they get older, losing the extreme energies of youth.

Jung sees the psyche not as a fixed, static entity, but as constantly changing and developing throughout life. A great deal of the work of personality development goes on at an unconscious level: on the whole we do not consciously choose to grow into a particular type of person. Throughout life we are influenced by our environment and the people we encounter on our journey. The behaviourist theory that was popular in Jung's time said that this was really all there was to it: the psyche was a blank slate at birth and developed gradually as a result of responses to external stimuli. Jung disagreed with this, saying that we are also born with a built-in human developmental programme, which is buried deep in the collective unconscious. Our journey of psychic development therefore follows a basic archetypal pattern, in much the same way as the physical body grows and develops in accordance with its genetic blueprint. This means that the conscious mind is only part of the picture and it is contained, like a smaller circle, within the larger circle of the unconscious.

Jung sees the individuation process as a basic biological process, present in all living organisms, not just in humans. In fact he saw it occurring even in inorganic systems, such as when a crystal forms a definite shape as it grows, suspended in a liquid solution. The goal of individuation is wholeness – a process of each individual organism becoming fully what it was intended to be from the beginning. In other words, for human beings it is a long process of becoming as complete and balanced a human being as we can.

Jung applied another basic biological principle to the psychology of the psyche: **the principal of homeostasis**. This refers to the way living organisms always strive to keep themselves in a state of balance, no matter what goes on in the environment. So, for example, when we are hungry we eat food, when we are too hot we take off clothes or seek a patch of shade. Again, this principle applies throughout the animal and plant kingdoms, and even within non-living systems. Jung always stressed that the psyche has evolved as a part of the world in which we live. Therefore he saw it as logical that the psyche too would seek balance at all times, just as the body does. Whenever a psychic process takes us too far in one direction, the psyche seeks to regulate the balance. Even the relation between conscious and unconscious has to operate on this same principle. This important theory of homeostasis within the psyche is what Jung refers to as the 'theory of compensation'. Once again Jung is describing dynamic opposites coming into action. Sometimes we seem to progress, and at other times, like Jung did during his midlife crisis, we seem to regress. All these stages are part of the growth of the psyche.

When we begin to pay more attention to our own psychic processes – perhaps by looking at our dreams, or starting psychoanalysis – the development of the personality becomes more conscious and deliberate. But Jung warns that the way is never straightforward and easy. At first, in fact, it may seem chaotic and endless and we feel that we are not getting anywhere. Only gradually do signs begin to appear that show us that we are getting somewhere on our quest. Interestingly, the path leads us in what seem like endless circles, and indeed Jung says that they are spirals – although we seem to keep coming back to the same place, we are actually further along the spiral. If we examine dream images over a period of time, we will find that the same kind of imagery comes up at repeated intervals.

The dreams rotate around a central key theme, drawing closer to the centre as we progress. Jung draws a parallel in nature with the growth of plants, which frequently show spiral patterns in their flowers and other growth areas. In fact the plant motif often occurs in dreams and is frequently drawn or painted spontaneously when people are undergoing analysis. Jung also found the tree symbol in alchemy, where it appears as the symbol of Hermetic philosophy, a system of thought originating in ancient Egypt, which had great influence on the Bible, the Quabalah, and Greek and Roman philosophy.

The individuation process is never complete: the spiral path takes us on a lifelong journey. As we travel we gradually unravel the conditioning imposed by our parents and society and peel away what Jung calls the 'false wrappings' of our persona. This frees us to meet our own shadow and acknowledge its power within us, so that we can try to stop projecting it onto others. Gradually, our psyche becomes more balanced and we are able to become much more whole and effective humans.

Archetypal stages of development

The archetypes are the structural elements or basic patterns of the collective unconscious, and the psychic health of the individual depends upon their proper functioning. As it develops, the individual ego-consciousness has to go through the same basic stages that occurred in the evolution of consciousness throughout the history of mankind. Jung found all these stages reflected in the imagery of myths. In the developing psyche this process normally goes ahead quite naturally, just as the physical body matures and grows naturally. During the course of this development, the different archetypes interact with one another in a similar way to that in which the physical organs of the body interact. The archetypes in charge of the stages of psychic development are only part of the whole archetypal reality.

Jung is frustratingly vague in describing an actual sequence of archetypal stages of development. He admitted that his ideas are bewildering and that he was constantly being sidetracked by new ideas. The task of making all his ideas into a coherent whole was later attempted by a student of Jung's, Erich Neumann, in his book *The Origins and History of Consciousness* (see **Further reading**). There is a foreword in this book by Jung, congratulating Neumann on his achievement and offering Neumann his 'heartfelt thanks' for his contribution to analytical psychology. Jung likens himself to a pioneer, exploring unknown territory and getting lost among endless new impressions and possibilities. Neumann, tracing Jung's footsteps, was able to follow the landmarks he had previously laid down. Jung saw Neumann's contribution as offering an evolutionary basis for his theories about the development of the human psyche, which would give a firm basis for future scientific research.

Neumann describes a sequence of archetypal events that occur on the hero's journey. It is useful to have a brief look at these, because similar ideas appear in various places throughout Jung's writing: as Jung says, he had done the groundwork and Neumann put it all together into a more logical sequence. Neumann's sequence begins and ends with the 'Uroboros', a serpent that eats its own tail, forming a circular motif. Jung was familiar with this symbol, as it occurs in various myths, as well as in alchemical literature. It symbolizes the creative and destructive aspects of nature, the endless cycle of life and death. The stages that the psyche follows through life are then described by Neumann as follows:

- world creation
- Great Mother
- separation of the World Parents
- birth of the Hero, i.e. the individual ego-consciousness – Jung placed this event at puberty
- slaying of the dragon
- rescue of the captive
- transformation and deification of the hero.

This sequence describes the whole life cycle, from birth to death. In his book *Man and his Symbols,* Jung describes a sequence that is similar to this in some ways. It shows four specific stages in the evolution of the hero, i.e. the development of the ego-consciousness. These stages are derived from the traditions of the Winnebago tribe of North America:

- Trickster represents the first and most primitive stage, where simple physical needs dominate behaviour. The infant has no purpose beyond gratifying these. His behaviour is cruel, self-seeking, cynical and unfeeling. This figure is often represented by an animal such as a sly fox.
- Hare represents the next stage, where the individual is starting to become socially adapted. The symbolic figure is

still an animal – in this case a hare, but elsewhere a coyote. This figure is often seen as the founder of human culture, even though he is still in animal form: he begins to modify the instinctual, infantile urges found in the Trickster cycle.

- **Red Horn** represents the third stage. He is the youngest of ten brothers and has to pass various archetypal tests, such as winning a race and proving his great strength. His companion thunderbird 'storms-as-he-walks' makes up for any shortcomings and weaknesses on the part of the hero. Red Horn represents the struggles of teens and young adulthood, where the growing psyche has to come to terms with living in the outer world.

- The final stage is represented by the **Twins**. These represent the dual aspect of man's nature – the basic struggle between opposites – and once again they are commonly found in mythology all over the world. Usually they are forced apart at birth and the mythical task is somehow to reunite them. This reflects the work that needs to be done in order to integrate the psyche – working on the shadow and so on.

Jung explored the archetypal stages mainly through looking at myths and legends in this way. He says that understanding these archetypal stories can help us to understand how the psyche develops, because the individual psyche mirrors the cultural evolution of consciousness that can be traced back through recorded history. The myth of the hero is the most commonly recurring myth throughout the world and it also crops up frequently in people's dreams. It varies enormously in its details, but the underlying theme is always similar, which suggests a universal archetypal pattern at work. For example, the hero has a miraculous but humble birth, shows early superhuman strength, rises rapidly in society, struggles with forces of evil, has human fallibility such as pride, and finally meets his death in the form of a human sacrifice through some sort of betrayal. A good example is found in the King Arthur myth. Jung says that this hero story has relevance for the development of individuals as they struggle to establish their own identity. It is also relevant for whole societies, as they establish their collective identity.

For Jung, the hero in all these stories represents the emerging ego-consciousness and its efforts to develop and grow. In his struggles, the hero often has help from divine figures and other guardians, who give him advice about how to get through all kinds of superhuman tasks that he cannot manage on his own. In the Arthur myth, for example, this figure appears in the form of Merlin. These superhuman figures are symbolic representations of the whole psyche, which, with its access to the world of the unconscious, can supply the missing information that the struggling ego lacks. The hero's final sacrificial death represents the achievement of maturity.

Like the mythical hero, we all encounter a new set of archetypal energies at each stage of our development. We need to integrate these, both in our personality and our behaviour. However, Jung points out that for most of his history man lived a simple hunter-gatherer existence, but recently we have evolved so fast that our archetypal pattern has not had time to catch up. This means that its programme is not always relevant to modern, mainly urban living. It does, however, equip us to follow the stages of growth basic to human beings all over the world: exploring our environment; learning who our family members are; learning family rules; getting to know the peer group; learning about social laws and beliefs; being initiated as an adult in society, and so on. All these stages are under the guidance of the Self. Other archetypal structures, such as those we looked at in the previous chapter – the ego, shadow, persona, animus and anima – also have their role to play in a person's psychic and social development.

Individuation and the Self

Unlike most psychologists of his day, Jung insisted that the development of the psyche extends well beyond childhood and adolescence, even continuing into old age: we never finish the process of self-examination and growth that charts our journey towards individuation. Jung believed that this process can never become complete unless the individual confronts the monsters that lurk in his own unconscious. He discovered these in his own psyche during his midlife crisis, and they appear throughout myth and legend in archetypal themes such as slaying the dragon.

Jung gave an analogy for the limited way in which most people live out their lives, saying that they only live on one or two floors of a large apartment building, never venturing into the rest. This building represents the psyche, where the unexplored rooms are the vast unexplored areas of the unconscious. Most people totally ignore their unconscious aspects, but if they can learn to listen to the messages that the unconscious brings in their dreams and fantasies, they can use them to enrich and heal their lives. The unconscious conveys these messages in the form of imagery, signs and symbols – it is up to the conscious mind to work with these in productive ways. This is not always easy because, as Jung discovered on his soul journey, the world of the unconscious is confusing and at times frightening.

The first layer that is usually uncovered when we begin to explore the unconscious is the shadow. As we saw in the previous chapter, this is made up of all the parts of ourselves that we don't really want to look at, or cannot consciously admit to – in other words, the aspects of ourselves that we do not like. The shadow is often projected outwards onto other people or groups of people. It can also be turned inwards and repressed, where it may cause neuroses or other psychic disturbances. Like all psychic elements, the shadow has both negative and positive aspects – the negative aspect can show us the darker sides of the personality and things that we need to work on. The positive aspect can show us qualities in ourselves that we have not acknowledged and which can be very empowering. Jung said that his own shadow was huge, and it was too big a task to tackle the whole of it in one lifetime. All he could do was to look at it and try to take responsibility for it.

Taking responsibility for our less favoured aspects is the first task of the Self in the individuation process. Throughout this process the psyche has to continually examine and confront what it produces. In terms of Jung's own two conflicting personalities, we could say that analytical, conscious personality Number 1 is continually looking at and trying to understand unconscious personality Number 2, which is always sending messages to try and get Jung's attention. The work is not easy, as Jung himself admitted, but it can have great rewards as it helps us to become more peaceful humans, better able to relate effectively to our fellow beings. That Jung himself largely achieved this daunting task is evident from the huge following he acquired later on in his life, having started out as a rather unpopular, bad-tempered youth.

Confronting the shadow is only the first task in the individuation process. Once we begin to know the shadow we reach the next layer in the psyche, which is the anima or animus – the opposite-sex image in the psyche. Once a man begins to understand and accept his anima it will help him towards achieving a balance between the inner and outer aspects of himself. We can see this in the way that Jung began to achieve a balance between his own inner and outer selves. Until his midlife crisis he had repressed the needs of personality Number

2. He then began to listen to his inner needs through creative play, building his tower at Bollingen, and seeking out the solitude he desperately needed.

The task for the woman is somewhat different. For her, understanding the energy of the supporting and guiding animus gives her a stronger structure on which to base her living. One of Jung's clients, writer Margaret Flinters, describes her own discovery of a ghostly figure somewhere inside her that directed her behaviour. This animus figure was based on her own father, who was a great perfectionist. Consequently she was always critical – her work was not good enough and her husband always fell short of her exacting ideal. In meeting Jung she encountered for the first time in her life a man who was more easy going and this helped to bring her down to earth.

Opposite-sex relationships present us with the stage on which we can explore all the different anima/animus energy, and this explains why they are frequently so difficult! If we are willing to grow together and help one another we can begin to achieve a mutual understanding. Jung says that the man's task here is to open his eyes to the psyche and the dark energies of the unconscious. Women on the other hand, who are naturally at home in the emotional and intuitive realms, have to find out how to function effectively in the outer world. It is interesting to speculate how all this will slowly change and evolve as the sex roles become less distinct in our modern world and as people begin to realize that we all have both male and female energies in our psyches.

We can begin to explore the world of the unconscious by means of dreams, because they represent ways in which the unconscious is trying to become conscious. Dreams reflect many of the processes going on in the unconscious, from simple everyday events that we may not have had time to assimilate fully, to exploring blocked-off shadow energy, right down to the numinous 'big dreams' that signal archetypal energies emerging from the collective unconscious. For more about dreams see Chapter 06.

Jung also used active imagination techniques to work further with dream contents and to begin to unravel and understand their deeper meaning. These techniques encourage a person to produce fantasy images that are very much like waking dreams and work in much the same way. Jung encouraged people to listen to the voice of the unconscious by first asking themselves who or what is trying to be heard and why. Having asked this question, one should then relax, try to switch off the endless babble of the conscious mind, and pay attention to whatever imagery or words arise from the inner world. Afterwards, one can write down whatever comes to mind. Images should be painted or drawn. The final task is to meditate on whatever one has produced in an uncritical manner, and to carry on developing the themes that arise. Jung stresses that the important thing here is always to let the unconscious take the lead, but never to allow it to take over completely – it is a question of achieving a healthy balance between the rational and intuitive aspects of the mind.

All these methods – confronting the shadow, working with the anima/animus, exploring dreams and fantasies – can help us to understand much about ourselves. It is important to try not to repress anything and to accept things as they really are. This may not be comfortable at times, and Jung says that the 'other' that we discover lurking within us may often seem alien and unacceptable. But our task is to stay with it and let the feelings sink in, because we will be richer for every little bit of self-knowledge. We have to accept the parts of ourselves that seem evil because they show us our areas of imbalance. Once we are able to take a good look at the conflicting opposites in our psyche it is possible to work towards the reconciling position that lies somewhere between the two. Jung found much to support this idea when he took up the study of alchemy – for more about this see Chapter 08.

The 'reconciling third' that appears when we integrate the positive and negative aspects of the psyche leads us to the goal, the inner core of our being, which Jung called the Self. He viewed this as a transpersonal, transcendent entity, and our final coming to it marks the end of the individuation process. The Self can appear in women's dream imagery as a high-priestess or goddess figure and in men's as a guru or nature spirit. It is also seen in many other images, such as the mandala, the famous philosopher's stone of alchemy, or in hermaphrodite figures. It always symbolizes wholeness and the completion of a cycle of living.

Jung saw the Self as being the most important aspect of the psyche. The ego merely serves as its mediator and protector, receiving and transmitting information, and observing progress. But, like all aspects of the psyche, even the Self has negative aspects that can lead to megalomania or possession. The important thing is always to seek and retain a sense of balance, connecting with both the inner and outer worlds.

Sex and gender

Psychologists have debated for many years as to whether 'nature' or 'nurture' has the greater effect upon our development of gender awareness. Are we born with a genetic blueprint that determines the way our psyche develops, or is it all to do with the way we are brought up? As we have already seen, Jung said that we are all born with a built-in archetypal pattern that gives us the blueprint for all aspects of psychic development. He agreed that environmental factors were very important too, but he did not believe that we begin with a totally blank slate. More recent studies in psychology and anthropology have tended to prove him right. For example, by the time a baby is born there are biological sex differences in size and weight and also in the ways in which we react to visual and auditory stimuli. This shows that there is indeed a biological blueprint at work from before birth.

As we grow up, we begin to create a persona that reflects the teachings of the society into which we were born. The animus or anima develops to compensate for this, incorporating the characteristics that we are not supposed to show publicly. In Jung's day the division between the two sexes was more marked than it is now, and so his anima showed markedly different behaviour from that of his persona. For example, men were supposed to be the bread winners and behave in an unemotional, logical fashion. Women were seen as being illogical, unpredictable and mysterious – which is just the way Jung's anima tended to behave.

Jung saw masculine and feminine as two major archetypal forces that coexisted as a balancing complementary pair of opposites. This idea is seen in myth and philosophical teachings all over the world, for example in the Chinese yin and yang (see the section on *I-Ching* in Chapter 08). These basic masculine and feminine principles are built into the psyche from birth, and it is upon these archetypal beginnings that personal gender awareness is built, beginning at a very early age. At first the child identifies with the mother, which causes a problem for the growing boy, who has to establish a gender identity that is opposite to that of the mother. If all goes well he will be able to transfer his gender identity to his father, or to other masculine figures. This enables him to learn how to function effectively in the outer world. Peer-group interactions are also vitally important in this process, and all children normally go through a stage before puberty where they interact almost exclusively with same-sex playmates.

For girls the problem is a different one – they do not have to break away from gender identification with the mother, because she is the same sex as they are. However, just like the boys, they are expected to develop a strong ego-identity and function in the outer world, gaining a good education and progressing on to earning a living. This means that they too have to follow the hero myth cycle. This is even truer today than it was in Jung's time, and yet the female superhero is still not as common in our mythology as her male counterpart. One only has to read children's books or watch films to see that this is true.

There is another problem for girls too, which Jung illustrates by referring to the fairy tale *Beauty and the Beast*. In this story the beast represents an older layer of the mind, an ancient, archetypal, animal energy (i.e. an erotic, sexual energy), which drives the woman towards biological fulfilment by giving birth to and mothering children. In order to do this she has to break the emotional and spiritual bond between herself and her father, because she has to seek a new man to be her mate. In the fairy tale, Beauty goes to live with the Beast in his castle, and is torn between loyalty to him and to her father, who subsequently falls ill. Frequently women resist the more primitive urge of the beast because it drives them away from the world of careers, competition, success and friendship in the outer world. This was even worse for women in Jung's day, when academic women and women with successful careers were frequently seen as being 'mannish' and rather sexless. In fact, women were frequently expected to abandon their careers altogether when they got married, because it was assumed that a woman's role would then be to bear children and look after the home.

Things are slow to change and even in the modern world there can still be enormous conflicts. These show not only in the psyche of the individual woman, but also in interactions with her man as they battle with the gender roles and arguments about who should do what around the home and in child-rearing. This is one example of the problems that Jung suggested our modern psyches will encounter when they try to develop along lines that have been laid down by thousands of years of evolution. He warns that our personal psychology is only skin deep, like a ripple on the ocean of the collective unconscious. Collective psychology is the most powerful force in our lives, the one that changes the world and makes history.

Rites of passage

Throughout life we all pass through different stages which bring change into our lives. Many of these changes, for example birth, marriage, childbirth, retirement and death, are marked by special ceremonies. These are so firmly established in the human psyche that many of them are archetypal: in more primitive societies, times of transition for the developing psyche were similarly marked by rites of passage. One of the most important ancient rituals, frequently neglected by modern society, is the initiation rite to mark puberty.

Jung says that all primitive groups and tribes that are at all organized have special rites of initiation to mark puberty. These are very important in the social and religious life of the tribe. Some of the rituals are very highly developed, but the underlying theme is always the same. Boys are usually isolated from their mothers and led away to special places where tribal elders initiate them into adulthood. Special rituals such as circumcision take place to emphasize their coming into manhood. Girls too are often taken to one side and instructed in the women's mysteries, such as menstruation and childbirth, by the wise older women. For both sexes the chief aim of these rites of puberty is to separate the young person from the parents, and mark a definite end to childhood.

In the childish stage of consciousness there are usually few problems for the psyche, because everything is taken care of by the parents. For Jung, puberty actually marks psychic birth, bringing with it a conscious distinction of the ego from the parents – the birth of the hero. From now onwards the demands of life put an end to the dreams of childhood and, if all goes well, the person will be able to make the transition to adulthood and independence. For others this stage is not easy and they soon run into problems, usually connected with sexual issues or a sense of inferiority. Jung says that although a huge variety of problems is encountered at this stage, they nearly always have one particular feature in common – that of clinging to the childhood level of consciousness in one way or another. People want to go on being unconscious, or at any rate be conscious only of the ego, rejecting everything foreign and indulging their own craving for pleasure or power.

Unfortunately, in the modern world initiation rites have either vanished altogether or turned into shadowy imitations, so that many people do not get any help in reaching maturity. Jung says that because of the archetypal roots deep in our psyche, we still need and crave ritual. Maybe our neglect of the initiation rite is one of the reasons so many people today seem to be finding it hard to enter adulthood fully.

Midlife crisis

As we approach middle age it often seems that we have got everything sorted out at last. Hopefully by now we have established our personal views and social positions, our careers and so on. But this is a point at which many people once more get stuck, assuming that their position is going to be eternally valid and clinging to their hard-won outlook. What they have overlooked is that unfortunately our achievements in society can only ever be won by focusing our awareness – a kind of narrowing down process. We have to concentrate on certain aspects of interest and push others away into a sort of psychic lumber room – there simply is not time or scope to do everything we would like to do!

Suddenly at the mid-point of our lives it dawns on us that time is beginning to run out. We still haven't been to Australia, won the Nobel Prize or travelled in outer space. This is the time of the midlife crisis, which Jung says is frequently marked in men by a period of depression around the age of 40, and at a slightly younger age in women. Once again, a significant change is being prepared for in the human psyche. This may appear as a slow change in a person's personality, or certain traits from childhood may re-emerge, or a person's interests may simply begin to change. Attitudes and beliefs may become more and more entrenched, until a person either becomes fanatical and bigoted, or else may have a sudden total change in their belief system. Jung describes the enchanting case of a very pious man he knew who was a churchwarden. He gradually grew more and more fanatical and intolerant about religious and moral matters, until by the time he was about 40 he had become 'a darkly lowering pillar of the church'. Then one night, when he was 55, he suddenly sat up in bed and announced to his wife that he had just realized he was actually 'a plain rascal'. Apparently he then spent his declining years in a feast of riotous living, wasting most of his accumulated fortune. Jung remarks that he was obviously 'quite a likeable person, capable of both extremes' (see *Modern Man in Search of a Soul* in **Further reading**).

Midlife crisis then, marks the return of the opposite, an attempt on the part of the psyche to re-balance itself. Jung says that this stage is actually very important, because otherwise we risk developing the kind of personality that attempts always to recreate the psychic disposition of youth. This is another way of getting stuck in looking to the past, in just the same way as some people get stuck at the childhood stage. Such a personality becomes wooden, boring and stereotyped.

Ageing

Jung says that the second half of life should have a very different quality from the first half. He compares the journey of the psyche to the daily journey of the sun, rising towards the zenith and then falling again. In the first half of life we are concerned with achievement, establishing ourselves in the world, earning a living, raising a family and so on. The problems we encounter are mainly biological and social. Later in life we can hopefully afford to become more inward looking and reflective. The problems we are involved with become more cultural and spiritual in nature. Confronting and integrating the repressed aspects of the personality may now lead eventually to the individuation of the psyche.

Jung says that the psychic changes that come with ageing tend to be reflected to some extent in the physical body. Women tend to develop more masculine features, such as deep voices and wispy moustaches. Men's voices often get thinner and higher, their faces soften and they tend to become plumper. Jung reports the case of a Native American chief, to whom Great Spirit appeared in a dream, announcing that from then on he must live with the women and children, wearing women's clothes and eating their food. This story illustrates the stage of life's decline, where our human values and even our bodies tend to undergo a reversal into the opposite.

In the realm of the psyche Jung observes a similar process going on. He says that it is as if we have a certain store of masculinity or femininity which by midlife is starting to run low, so we then allow our unused opposite-sex energy to come into play. He gives the example of a middle-aged man who, feeling tired of work, winds up his business. His wife then takes over and perhaps opens a little shop, where he potters around being the handyman. Very often these role reversals are accompanied by upheavals in the marriage as the husband discovers his emotional side at last, and the wife her sharp and logical mind.

Jung warns that we cannot live the afternoon of life as we did the morning: what was great in the morning will be seen to be little in the evening, and what was true in the morning will become a lie. At this stage it is essential to begin to explore the world within the psyche if we wish to stay psychologically healthy; we must begin to understand ourselves and our spiritual nature. But this is not always easy, and many people prefer to get stuck in the past, perhaps becoming endlessly moaning victims, tedious eternal adolescents, or stuffy boring old doctrinaires.

Jung suggests that the first half of life is really concerned with nature – gaining a reputation, earning a living, raising a family. The second half of life can then be seen as concerned with culture. In primitive societies, it is almost always the old people who are the guardians of the mysteries and the laws that express the cultural heritage of the tribe. So what is going on in our modern society, with its cult of youth that makes older people frantically try to stay young forever? Where do the old people fit in? What has happened to their precious wisdom and vision?

It is important at each stage of life to be able to look forward, and this is where religious beliefs can become very important, because they offer people a continuation of life, something greater to look forward to. Jung points out that it is impossible for us to know what happens to us after death. That being said, however, he says that a directed life is generally richer and healthier than an aimless one, and it is always better to go forwards with the stream of time. For this reason he views religious belief in some kind of afterlife as healthy, because it gives people the feeling of safety and security that enables them to keep on moving forward. He explains that because of the archetypes that make up the basis of the human psyche, we need beliefs of this sort rather as our bodies need salt: in other words, they are basic to our psychic well-being.

With old age the psyche reaches the final stage in its cyclical journey. The first stage was childhood, where we are a problem to others, but not yet conscious of self-responsibility. Next came youth and middle age, with its conscious problems. The final stage is extreme old age, when we often once again become a problem for others. Although childhood and old age are very different stages, they have in common a submersion in the world of the unconscious, into which we must all ultimately vanish.

Summary

- The psyche is not a fixed, static entity, but changes and develops throughout life.
- It works on biological principles which are basic to the natural world and which provide it with its driving force.
- The journey of the psyche follows universal archetypal patterns that are reflected in rites of passage.
- In order to achieve individuation it is important for us always to move forward with the flow of our lives and not to get stuck in previous stages of development.

06

dreams and symbols

In this chapter you will learn:
- why dreams are so important in understanding the psyche
- where dreams come from
- how we can analyse our dreams and use them for personal development.

The importance of dreams

Dreams were enormously important to Jung throughout his life and they are one of the key aspects of Jungian analysis. For Jung dreams, archetypes and other mental imagery have a separate psychic reality of their own, just as our thoughts have: they may give us valuable insights that 'we' would never have thought of. He did not claim to understand how this worked – in fact he said that he had no dream theory and did not know where they came from. However, Jung suggests various different functions that dreams serve:

• to act as compensation for areas of the conscious mind that are deficient or distorted in some way

• to bring back archetypal memories from the collective unconscious

• to draw attention to both inner and outer aspects of our lives of which we are not consciously aware.

Jung's ideas about dreams were very much influenced by Freud. It was Freud who had first realized the value of dreams as tools for exploring the psyche, and his theories gave Jung a starting point for exploring and developing theories of his own. This time it was Freud who was the pioneer, and Jung who built further upon what he had discovered. Freud saw dreams as neurotic symptoms, probably because nearly all his patients were in fact neurotic. He said that dreams are symbolic wish fulfilments of desires that have been repressed. These desires are mostly sexual. By exploring the hidden desire symbolized in a dream one could begin to unravel a person's neurosis. In its simplest form, a dream directly expresses a wish, for example a person who is hungry will dream of food. Freud saw dreaming largely as being a form of regression to childhood and the instinctive forces and images that dominate this time of our lives. In fact, he thought they were mostly manifestations of infantile sexual urges. Because these urges were unacceptable they were suppressed and so the dream is a censored way of expressing what has been long buried. According to Freud, recent events and desires in a person's life hold a minor role in dreams – they usually only appear if they somehow trigger one of the early repressed desires.

Freud's theory was that dreams allow the impossible to happen, and set aside the normal inhibitions of waking life. During sleep, forbidden wishes rise from the unconscious where they are normally kept under control during waking hours. As they attempt to come into the conscious mind, the brain monitors them and decides that they have disturbing content and must therefore be suppressed for fear they disturb the sleeper. Dreams are then created in order to express the hidden wishes in a disguised form, so that the person can go on sleeping. So dreams are seen by Freud as guardians, allowing us to sleep peacefully.

Jung felt that a dream always has an underlying idea or intention – it is expressing something important that the unconscious wants to say. A dream shows a person's inner truth and reality, not necessarily as that person would wish it to be, but as it really is. Jung said that Freud's theory was far too simplistic and the idea that dreams were simply imaginary fulfilments of repressed wishes was totally out of date. Jung thought that the concerns expressed in dreams were much more wide-ranging – they may contain truths, wild fantasies, memories, hopes and fears, even telepathic imagery and much more. For Jung, a dream is an important message from the unconscious that can act as a key to helping a person with their individuation process.

Freud used dreams as important starting points for triggering off a free-association process. He would pick out a particular symbol in a patient's dream and see where the associated train of thought led. Jung felt that this approach was rather limited for several reasons:

- it debases the rich symbolism and imagery contained in many dreams
- it often leads one off on another path entirely, away from the original meaning of the dream
- the dream expresses something that the unconscious is trying to convey. Therefore it is more important to look at the actual content of the dream, rather than spinning off at a tangent and analysing its separate components as Freud was inclined to do.

Jung was urging that we listen to what the individual person has to say, and treat the dream as something unique to that person. In order to know and understand a person's whole personality and psychic reality it is vital to realize that dreams and symbolic imagery have a very important role to play. Jung saw this insight as a turning point in his understanding of human psychology.

Jung agreed with Freud when he said that dreams often arose from emotional upsets, in which complexes were frequently involved. These complexes were like tender spots in the psyche that easily reacted to external stimulus or disturbance. However, Jung pointed out that one can also explore complexes by means of word-association tests, meditation or conversation – they do not have to wait to be uncovered by a dream.

Freud explained that dreams have a 'manifest' content (which is what the dream appears to be about) and a 'latent' content (which is the dream's true, hidden meaning). Finding this hidden meaning will therefore unlock the secrets of the psyche. Jung could not agree that dreams were just covering up suppressed material. He said that what Freud called the manifest content was actually the whole meaning of the dream. It was expressed in symbolic form simply because the unconscious operates in symbols and so tries to convey its ideas to our conscious minds in this way. Because the conscious mind tends to think in words rather than symbols, we need to translate the symbolic content of our dreams into a form we can more readily understand.

Their different approach to theories about dreams was another key factor in the rift that finally came between Freud and Jung. Eventually, Jung agreed to differ with Freud and developed his own ideas, but as with his theories about the development of the psyche, he never really set out a cut-and-dried theory about dreams as Freud had tried to do. He was not even sure that his way of working with dreams could be counted as a 'method'. This did not mean, however, that he did not consider dreams to be of paramount importance in the individuation process.

Symbols

Freud believed that much of a dream's content was disguised by means of symbols. Freudian symbols within dreams have become one of the most well-known aspects of psychoanalytic thinking. Freud believed that symbols had fixed meanings common to all humans, and therefore under certain circumstances it was possible to interpret a dream without actually questioning the dreamer – provided one knew a bit about the dreamer's personality, life circumstances, and the impressions that preceded the occurrence of the dream. Jung was also interested in the symbolism that appeared in dreams, but for him the symbols produced by the unconscious mind had much deeper meaning than Freud had believed. Jung decided that the strange mythological fragments that appeared in his own dreams and fantasies and those of his patients were rich in archetypal symbolism. He found that they were often highly numinous in character and therefore he felt that they were very important for the growth of the psyche. In fact, Jung did not believe that Freudian symbols were actually symbols at all – they were merely 'signs' used to represent something already known about and universally recognizable, for example a pointy stick is a penis, a cave is a vagina and so on.

Unlike a sign, a symbol is a term, a name or an image that contains special associations in addition to its obvious everyday meaning. For example, a rainbow can be a symbol for joy and hope of good things to come. Symbols often occur spontaneously in dreams and also crop up as symbolic thoughts, acts and even situations. Sometimes inanimate objects are involved in symbolic events, for example the clock that symbolically stops when someone dies.

Many symbols are not just meaningful for the individual but for society as a group. These are often religious symbols such as the ox, lion, man and eagle, which represent the four evangelists in the Christian religion. Animals very often crop up as religious symbols: in Egyptian mythology, for example, the gods are represented as having attributes of animals such as the jackal, hawk, cat and so on. This type of symbolism is used to express ideas that are beyond words. The origin of typical religious symbols is often attributed to the gods themselves, but Jung says that they actually arise from spontaneous primeval dreams and fantasies.

Jung viewed dreams as fantasies that arise during sleep and said that a similar process goes on unconsciously even while we are awake, especially when we are under the influence of repressed or unconscious conflicts. A good deal of our perception of reality goes on at a subconscious level, because we are so bombarded with stimuli all the time that we could not possibly register everything that goes on around us. This means that we actually perceive many more events than we register consciously. Sometimes these events well up from the subconscious later on – perhaps in a moment of intuition or in a dream. We then realize that they hold emotional meaning or other significance.

Jung says that dream symbols are mostly manifestations of the area of the psyche that lies beyond the control of the conscious mind. He likens the way in which the psyche spontaneously produces symbols to the way in which a plant produces its flower. Dreams are therefore seen by Jung as evidence of natural psychic activity and growth, rather than the neurotic symptoms that Freud believed they were. They help the psyche to resolve conflicts and to understand things in a new light; their symbolic content has a transcendent quality that helps the psyche towards healing and wholeness. This was so important to Jung that he considered working with symbols to be one of the key factors in analysis and always encouraged people to play creatively with the symbols that arose spontaneously in their dreams and fantasies and develop them further.

The origins of dreams

Jung regarded dreams as totally natural phenomena not under the control of the will. He explained that they always seek to express something which the conscious mind does not understand properly. There can be many different reasons for dreams, and Jung considers possible causes, including:

- **physical causes,** such as having eaten a huge meal before going to bed
- **memory recall,** which may be from the distant past, or just mulling over events from the previous day
- **compensations** for things that one lacks in waking life. Such a dream may highlight a hidden wish or conflict. Recurring dreams are often attempts to compensate for particular defects in a person's attitude to life. Such conflicts may date from childhood
- **looking ahead,** including warning dreams and those where we worry about forthcoming events, as well as the more mysterious precognitive dream. Crises in our lives often have a long unconscious history before they actually happen. Recurring dreams may also fall into this category
- **Oracular dreams,** also called 'big' dreams by Jung. These are dreams that feel numinous and highly significant to the dreamer – the sort of dream that our ancestors would have interpreted as messages from the gods. They are sometimes precognitive.

Jung agreed with Freud that dreams were partly woven from material from childhood and also from recent events in the dreamer's life, but he also began to realize that there was a third source. Just as the human embryo develops through the stages of its evolutionary history, so the mind travels on its own evolutionary journey. Dreams therefore allow recall of past memories, right back into childhood and beyond, to the most primitive instincts from the collective unconscious. As Freud had already recognized, recall of past events can be very healing in some cases, filling in gaps in memory from infancy and bringing balance or enrichment to the adult psyche. The further a person goes into analysis, the more complex and symbolic their dreams tend to get. Jung saw that they may begin to extend beyond personal life and its experiences, into the realm of the collective and mythological. But he never lost sight of the fact that he saw them as natural products that contributed to the overall balance of the psyche, working on the biological principles of homeostasis and survival of the individual.

Archetypes in dreams

Jung stressed that it is important to understand the individual in the context of mankind's psychic history, as well as looking at his or her own life experience. This means that the analyst needs to have a good grasp of mythology as well as experience with personal dreams. Archetypal images and figures that appear in dreams are not the archetype itself, they are simply representations of it. For example, a dream of the Virgin Mary might be one way of representing the divine mother, or goddess archetype, which is a basic pattern built into the human brain. These archetypal patterns are closely connected to human instincts. Instincts are physiological urges that can be perceived by the normal senses, but they can also manifest as symbolic images – these are the archetypes. In other words, the archetype gives a definite form to the energy of the instinct, which makes it easier for us to understand.

Jung says that dreams often work in a compensatory way, following the homeostatic principle. If our psychic energy sways too far one way then an archetypal image may be produced in our dreams to show us where the imbalance lies. This is the means by which the unconscious gets through to the ego. So when we begin to analyze a dream, it is often helpful to ask ourselves what conscious attitude it compensates for. For example, if we are feeling left out and needy in some way then we might dream of a divine mother archetype who is giving us food. She might appear as our own mother, or perhaps as a cook or a dinner lady.

Jung's idea of discovering and freeing balancing energies in this way seems much more relevant than Freud's reductive method of boiling dreams down to images that mask childhood sexual trauma. It enables us to work with the present and the future, rather than merely unravelling the past. Interestingly, archetypes quite often appear in children's dreams, such as Jung's own phallus dream. Jung gives an example of a whole series of dreams recorded and drawn by a ten-year-old girl. The archetypal content in these dreams is very strong, and as far as Jung was able to discover, was not related to any mythological ideas or religious beliefs that her family held. This supports Jung's idea that the archetypes are inborn in us.

Analysing dreams

For Jung, a dream was a complex intuitive structure, which must be viewed as a whole, rather than being picked apart. The idea, therefore, is not to interpret the dream, so much as to amplify it by looking at the imagery in it and identifying the general mood and feelings associated with it. Each image in the dream needs to be considered in turn, always looking at it within the context of the dreamer's own life. For example, supposing someone dreams that they are using a stick to beat down a door – for Freud this would be an obvious sexual symbol, with the stick representing a phallus; but Jung pointed out that it could mean something else entirely. The unconscious has deliberately chosen this particular symbol and the analyst's task is to find out why.

Even common dream themes such as falling and flying must be viewed in terms of the dream itself. Each dream arises from the individual psyche, in answer to specific circumstances and emotions. It is not possible, therefore, to lay down general rules for dream interpretation and we should be careful never to impose a meaning on somebody else's dream. We can never fully understand another person's dream and so it is vital to keep our own flow of associations in check. So:

• the dream should always be treated as a *fact*, we should make no previous assumptions about it

• the dream is a specific creation from the unconscious that somehow makes sense, even if we cannot immediately see how

• we should explore the content of the dream thoroughly to try and find out what unconscious message is trying to emerge.

Jung emphasizes that because symbols always convey more than is immediately apparent, it is important not to reduce them down to a single meaning. Instead, we should stay with them, meditating upon different aspects of their meaning, and always taking into account what they mean to the individual.

Dreams have a tendency to occur in series, with each separate dream conveying the underlying message in a slightly different way. Jung found that as a rule a series of dreams was more useful for interpretation than a single dream. This is because important points become clearer with repetition, and mistakes in interpretation are often corrected by analysing a subsequent dream. Not only that, but we can also observe progress as the psyche slowly resolves the problem it is working with.

A dream can be approached in various different ways:

- **Objectively** – the dream is considered in terms of the person's real life in the external world. For example, if you dream that your car has broken down, the dream may be telling you that it is time to take your car in for a service.

- **Subjectively** – the dream is considered in terms of what it represents within the person's own personality. This time the car might represent yourself – perhaps there is a hidden health problem nagging away at your unconscious mind and it's time for a visit to the doctor.

- **Collectively** – if the dream contains numinous, archetypal symbols then we can look towards the collective unconscious and mythological interpretations. This time the car might represent a vehicle that is taking you on your life's journey, so the dream is pointing out that you need to give attention to your spiritual progress.

Of course, many of our dreams are only remembered in small snippets, but Jung said that some can be recalled as a whole story that can be looked upon as a little private drama. He sometimes found it helpful to break the story down into four stages:

- **Exposition** – this is like the beginning of the play, or the prologue. It sets the scene and introduces the main characters.

- **Development of the plot** – this is a tool used by all successful writers to build up the suspense and make us wonder what is going to happen.

- **Culmination** – at this point something decisive happens, or a complete change occurs.

- **Lysis** – this is the conclusion or solution. It is sometimes only reached later on, by working with the dream.

Breaking the dream down into stages in this way may help us to understand the dream more fully. We can begin to ask questions, such as why the dream was set where it was, and why certain characters appear in it. It is also interesting to observe sequences of dreams where the same setting and characters appear but in slightly different ways. This can point to the unconscious trying to get closer and closer to the centre of an issue and presenting it from different angles. The point of culmination may be quite different in subsequent dreams in a series as we get closer to the truth of the matter.

Jung's house dream

Jung gives an example of a dream that he had about a house and uses it to describe some of the possible pitfalls of interpreting another person's dream. In this dream he was exploring a house on various different levels. He began on the first floor, which was furnished in the style of the eighteenth century. Below this the ground floor was dark and appeared to be furnished more in sixteenth-century style. The lower he went into the house, the more primitive the floors became, until the bottom cellar was Roman. In the floor of the cellar was a stone slab, which revealed the way down to a cave full of prehistoric bones and skulls.

When Jung analyzed this dream he realized that it was a sort of summary of his own life. He grew up in a house that was about two hundred years old, and his parents' attitude was in many ways medieval. The lower levels illustrated his passionate interest in ancient history and palaeontology. However, when Jung discussed this dream with Freud, Freud became obsessed with the image of the skulls. He kept returning to them over and over, insisting that Jung try to find a wish in connection with them. Jung soon realized that Freud was hinting at a hidden death wish.

Jung concluded that this was his dream, about his own private world. This was important because he came to understand that dream analysis is not a technique that can be learned and applied by following strict rules – it has to be done by means of discussion between two people. The danger is always that the analyst's interpretation might dominate that of the patient. Jung gave up using hypnosis for the same reason – it gave the therapist too much control over the patient.

Sometimes a dream or vision cannot be understood however much one tries to investigate it. Jung says that it is best then to leave it in the back of one's mind because it may become clearer at a later date. Often an external event will clarify a dream that one has been mulling over. Jung says that if one carries a dream around for long enough some sense will always emerge from it.

For Jung, dreams and symbols are never pointless or meaningless. On the other hand they are often not connected directly with worldly concerns, which is why many people tend to dismiss them as being unimportant. Jung says that to him it is incredible that although we get messages from our unconscious psyche almost every night, most people cannot be bothered to explore their meaning, and often even mistrust or despise them. He wonders, in fact, what the unconscious thinks of us! Jung was never able to agree with Freud that a dream is merely a façade, behind which lurks a meaning that is already known but is being withheld from consciousness. Dreams for Jung are often difficult to understand because they are expressed in symbols and pictures, which form the language of the unconscious. They are not deliberately deceptive, they are simply natural attempts by the unconscious to express ideas in its own way.

Summary

- Dreams were very important to Jung throughout his life and took a central place in his new psychology.
- A dream is personal to the individual and can help with the individuation process. Interpretation should be carried out by means of talking to the dreamer about the actual dream itself.
- The dream can arise from many different sources, but it always has a meaning that is relevant to the dreamer.
- Dreams are not just about hidden wish fulfilments. They can reflect many different aspects of the life of an individual and can also extend beyond the individual psyche into the world of the collective unconscious.
- The analyst needs to have a good grasp of mythological ideas so that dreams can be looked at in a collective context when archetypal material emerges.
- It is often helpful to look at a whole series of dreams that have a connecting theme, because this will lead to fresh insights.

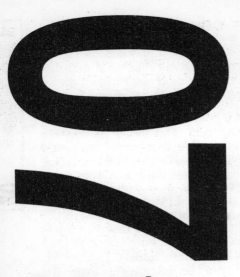

07

the personality and relationships

In this chapter you will learn:
- key facts about Jung's theory of personality
- how the individual personality develops
- the influence our psychological type has on our social life.

The psychology of consciousness

Jung was interested in studying the conscious aspects of the mind as well as the unconscious, but he pointed out that any study of the human mind is difficult to carry out scientifically. In any other science it is possible to apply a hypothesis to an impersonal subject. In psychology, however, one inevitably comes up against the fact that it is a case of one psyche studying another, or worse still, studying itself. This means that human relationships and the personality of the investigator always get in the way. This is particularly true when an analyst is working with a patient: no matter how impersonal the analyst tries to be, once he or she is fully engaged in conversation with the patient it is impossible not to bring subjective factors in.

Jung felt that a broad understanding of the different ways in which people relate to the world would help analysts and their patients towards understanding the dynamics of their relationships. This was one of the main reasons that he was interested in developing a theory about different types of human personalities, which he called his 'psychology of consciousness'. He also explained that if one was made aware of the strengths in one's psyche, one could then begin to work on the weaker areas, and so achieve more balance. Jung observed that human behaviour tends to follow certain basic patterns, which often operate as pairs of opposites. During the course of development, one emphasis often comes to be preferred, so the person tends to develop that mode of behaviour and act according to its characteristic aspects. The preferred mode of behaviour gradually becomes habitual and leads to predictable personality traits and ways of behaving.

Jung eventually developed a theory of psychological types that is still used today in modified forms. It was Jung who first gave us the well-known idea that people could be 'introverts' or 'extroverts'. These are what he called the two 'attitude' types. He explained that this way of dividing people into groups is only one of many possible generalizations, but it helps people to understand themselves and one another. For example, it can highlight difficulties that commonly arise if a patient belongs to one group and the analyst to another. Jung later decided that the two attitude types were too broad and general, so he added four 'functions' – thinking, feeling, sensation and intuition.

A person's personality is made up of any combination of the two attitude types and the four functions. The two attitude types are:

- **introversion** – the psychic energy is turned inwards, towards the subject
- **extroversion** – the psychic energy is turned outwards, towards the object.

The four functions are:

- **thinking** – this type of person relates to the world via logic and the intellect
- **feeling** – this type makes value judgements about the world
- **sensation** – this type relies mainly on sensory impressions
- **intuition** – this type perceives the world mainly through the unconscious.

A person is basically either introvert or extrovert, and their primary function can be any of the four described above. But the personality is not fixed – it is possible and even desirable to develop opposite characteristics and functions in order to become more balanced.

As is the case with all Jung's theories, his theory of psychological types was too complex to have emerged fully formed all at once, and he was constantly working on it and modifying it. In 1921 he published a large and complicated volume called *Psychological Types,* in which he attempted to explain his theory. But the origins of his ideas about personality went back a long time before this. As early as 1904, when he was working with patients at Burghölzi on word-association tests, he began to sort their responses into two large groups which he called 'egocentric' and 'impersonal'. Originally he related these to the psychiatric classifications of hysteria and schizophrenia, but he soon realized that they could have wider implications for general psychology. In 1913, he delivered a paper to the 4th International Psychoanalytic Congress in Munich, entitled 'A Contribution to the Study of Psychological Types', which outlines some of the theories he was later to expand upon in *Psychological Types.*

Between 1918 and 1920 Jung had begun to realize that for him the goal of psychic development was individuation – the finding of the Self. *Psychological Types* is an attempt to provide some sort of framework for people to work with in the individuation process. When the book was first translated into English in 1923 by H. G. Baynes, it had an added subtitle, *The Psychology of Individuation.* This was a subtitle that had actually been suggested by Jung, and it reflects his main purpose in trying to formulate a theory of personality.

Introversion and extroversion

Jung's theory divided people into two basic types according to the orientation of their psychic energy, or libido. The two different attitudes were called introversion and extroversion and the two psychological types introverts and extroverts. These terms are so well known today that people take them for granted in everyday use of language. Everyone has both attitudes to varying degrees, but there is a tendency for one of them to dominate.

- **Introverts** withdraw psychic energy from the world and direct it towards the 'subject' – they are more interested in their own inner world of thoughts and feelings than the external world. Their behaviour is governed mainly by subjective factors. They are reflective, hesitant people, with retiring natures, preferring to keep themselves to themselves and disliking large groups. They are cautious, often shrinking away from new objects and situations, and may appear to be somewhat on the defensive. Introverts need privacy and personal space and spend a lot of their time in contemplation. An extreme form of introversion appears in autism and some types of schizophrenia.

- **Extroverts** direct their psychic energy outwards towards the external world. They naturally give their greatest attention to the 'object' – they are interested in the external world and relationships, and their behaviour tends to be governed by objective factors. They are outgoing and frank, with accommodating, adaptable personalities. Extroverts need action and other people around them. Extreme extroverts are not happy with their own company: they cannot bear silence and solitude and need constant excitement and stimulation from others in order to prevent boredom or depression from setting in.

Jung realized that nobody ever fitted exactly into one type. People have an infinite variety of different personalities and it would be too narrow and simplistic to fit them neatly into two categories. Because we all possess both attitudes, it is more a question of whether one predominates over the other. Jung's theory is not really attempting to explain *individual* psychology – it is a generalization, aimed at trying to explain human behaviour by looking at what people have in common. Usually one or other attitude will dominate the personality and the other attitude becomes unconscious. The psyche will then find compensatory ways of expressing this hidden attitude. The two types of attitude tend to clash because where the extrovert will follow the crowd, the introvert will deliberatley reject the majority view. The introvert likes peace and solitude, whereas the extrovert likes to be active and sociable. Each type tends to despise and undervalue the other. So the introvert sees the extrovert as brash and noisy, often shallow and critical; whereas the extrovert thinks the introvert is self-centred and tends to see all that inward reflection as pointless, even morbid. As a pair the two types follow the law of opposites, so if a person is an extreme type, the opposite type will tend to emerge at some point – an amusing example is given in Jung's story about the churchwarden in Chapter 05.

Jung attempts to base his two psychological types firmly in biology, pointing out that the relation between subject and object is always to do with adaptation to the environment. He says that in nature there are two main ways of adapting:

- by increased fertility, at the expense of individual defence and preservation
- by increased self-protection, at the expense of fertility.

Jung sees this biological contrast as the basis for his two psychological types of adaptation. The extrovert has a constant urge to use his energy in the external world, whereas the introvert concentrates on defending himself and conserving his energy.

The four functions

The idea of there being four balanced elements within nature is very old. Shamanic and magical traditions often use a system where four elements – earth, air, fire and water – are related to four directions – north, east, south and west. Each element is also associated with different corresponding energies that are often represented symbolically by animals, plants, seasons, colours and so on. For example, south is usually associated with the fire element, so an appropriate animal might be a dragon, the colour could be red and the season summer.

Long ago in Ancient Greece, doctors and philosophers began to identify four personality types, based on the same idea of four balanced natural energies. These types, or 'humours', were called melancholic, sanguine, choleric and phlegmatic. Jung developed his theory of four personality functions based on a similar idea. His four functions are grouped as two opposite

The four functions

pairs, giving them a feeling of balance. He named the four functions thinking, feeling, sensation and intuition. Thinking and feeling are opposites, as are sensation and intuition. If one function is more developed in a person, then its opposite will be correspondingly underdeveloped and even repressed. For example, an intellectual, thinking person who is always 'living in the head' might have difficulty in the feeling areas – expressing emotion and coming 'from the heart'. Similarly, a person with a more developed sensation function relies on stimuli from the outer world and tends to ignore the inner 'gut feelings' of intuition.

Thinking

This it is to do with rational analysis – it tells you what something is. Thinking people have logical, probing and questioning minds. They are good at seeing cause and effect, judging things and reaching logical conclusions by using their intellect and connecting ideas. They are frank and may appear cool and distant emotionally. This kind of person is good at adapting to new circumstances. Examples of this type are the scientist and the philosopher.

Feeling

This tells you whether something is agreeable to you or not. Feeling people make judgements about how they value things, assessing them on whether they are 'pleasant' or 'unpleasant', 'good' or 'bad' and so on. The word 'feeling' is not a very good choice really and it has led to a lot of confusion. Jung eventually realized this and tried to clarify what he meant, saying that he used the word 'feeling' to refer to a rational function, used for putting things in order of value. He did not use it to refer to emotional feeling, which can be associated with any of the four functions. 'Evaluating' or 'assessing' might have been better words to use. Feeling people have a strong sense of traditional values, and human relationships are important to them. They are often warm, creative people.

Sensation

By sensation Jung means sense perception. This tells you that something exists in the outer world and gives information about what it is like. This kind of person relies very much upon conscious sensory impressions, perceived through the sense organs. They assess their world by how things look, what words sound like and so on. Material things are very important to them and they are solid, grounded people. They take everything at face value and 'call a spade a spade'. They can be boring and plodding, lacking in imagination, but on the other hand they are often jolly and easygoing. Their calm nature makes them appear rational and practical, but this is not always the case, and at its most negative this type may be crudely sensual.

Intuition

This gives you hunches about things. It tells you where something comes from and where it is going. It differs from sensation in that it does not rely on the known sense organs and seems to have no physical cause. This kind of person is aware of chances, possibilities, the past and the future. They are often unaware of their own bodies and may be dreamy and ungrounded. They can become impatient with solid, monotonous detail and they are not practical people. Intuitive people are able to perceive possibilities that are not known consciously through the normal senses. Intuition is the source of creativity and inspiration.

Thinking and feeling are both seen by Jung as rational functions, because they are ordering functions that involve making judgements and evaluations about the world. Intuition and sensation he calls 'irrational'. Again, this is a misleading word to use as it seems to imply that they are illogical or deranged in some way. But Jung does not mean to imply this – he uses the word to describe processes that depend on objective stimuli which owe their existence to physical causes rather than mental ones.

Again, Jung points out that the four functions represent only one possible way of classifying human behaviour. There are many others, such as will power, memory and imagination. He said that he did not intend to be dogmatic about them: he was simply presenting them as a helpful tool in explaining parents to children, husbands to wives and so on, and also in understanding and overcoming one's own prejudices.

A person's conscious orientation will usually be towards one of the four functions. This dominant function is called the 'principal function' and it will determine how the person reacts to experiences. There is usually a second function that is mainly conscious, and this is called the 'auxiliary function'. A third function, the opposite of the auxiliary function, is slightly suppressed and partially unconscious. The last function, which is the opposite of the principal function, remains largely unconscious. When the conscious function is particularly strong there is a tendency for the opposite function to break through into consciousness now and again. This is called 'the return of the repressed' and it may manifest as hysteria, phobias, obsessions, unbalanced moods and so on. In order to gain a balanced, healthy mental attitude it is often necessary to work with the repressed function in therapy.

The eight psychological types

Each of the four functional kinds of personality may be extroverted or introverted. Jung therefore combined the four functions and the two attitudes, to arrive at eight psychological types. A person's psychological type is important in determining their view of the world and how they cope with situations and relationships.

The extroverted thinking type

This type is dominated by rational thinking and logic. They always direct their libido outwards, towards practical outcomes, basing all their thinking and actions on analysis of objective data. They love order and facts and are good at problem solving and clarifying issues. They tend to think that their view of the world is the correct one, so they may become tyrants. In fact, they conveniently suppress anything that doesn't fit in with their world-view. Their opposite, or 'shadow', type is the introverted feeling type. Because they repress the feeling function they are not very good at personal relationships and they tend to scorn religious ideas. What they repress may return as violent moods, wild love affairs and petty, bigoted behaviour towards those who threaten their world-view. They have a strong sense of duty but they may lack warmth and tolerance. Many scientists, lawyers, technicians, administrators and engineers may belong to this type.

The introverted thinking type

This type is also interested in intellectual ideas, but is orientated more towards the inner world of ideas than external facts. These people are by nature contemplative: they constantly ask questions and formulate theories about things, but they are reserved about accepting 'facts'. Their thinking is directed inwards, towards subjective ideas, and they are not particularly interested in practical outcomes. They may appear eccentric and impractical to others and may be so cut off from the world that relationships are unimportant to them. Their shadow type is the extroverted feeling type. The repressed feeling function makes it hard for them to share their feelings with others. It may surface in the form of childish naivety or strange unpredictable behaviour and they may interpret criticism of their ideas as personal attack. Philosophers and intellectuals may belong to this type, and Jung is once said to have put himself into this category when talking to a colleague.

The extroverted feeling type

This type is well adjusted to the world around them and fits in well with their peer group. This is very important to them, because their thinking is based on traditional social values. They are conventional, outgoing people, close followers of fashion, and much concerned with personal success. They are tactful and charming, handling people well, and enjoy social gatherings and groups. The shadow type is the introverted thinking type, which can lead to an unconscious way of thinking that is infantile, archaic and negative. This means that on the negative side they can be rather shallow, insincere and posing, and in extreme cases may develop hysteria or mania. This group may include actors, people in PR work or marketing and TV stars.

The introverted feeling type

This type is rather remote and inward looking, the 'still waters run deep' type of person. They are reserved and enjoy peace and quiet, poetry and music, tending to undervalue objective reality. They prefer to have a few intimate friends and they understand people close to them quite well. They are often very religious and self-sacrificing. These people are usually very genuine because they are hopeless at role-playing, so they make loyal friends. The shadow type is the extroverted thinking type, so this group may not be able to think things through logically and may get caught up in primitive obsessions or depression. Monks and nuns may belong to this group, and its extreme form is shown in the mystical, ecstatic character who totally turns away from the world.

The extroverted sensation type

For this type, physical objects and sensations in the outside world are very important. This is the practical, man-of-the-world type who accepts the world as it is and enjoys living in it. They enjoy such things as good food or dangerous sport, and are good entertainers. The libido is directed towards objects and activities that arouse strong sensations that are usually, but not always, pleasurable. They are not interested in the inner world and are suspicious of people who look at things in terms of psychological processes. The shadow type is the introverted intuitive type and this can give rise to unfounded negative obsessions. This type can be addictive and pleasure seeking and extreme cases have a tendency towards perversion, or joining weird cults. Their repressed intuitive side may also be projected onto others, so that they can be irrationally suspicious or jealous in their behaviour. People of this type are often in business or property dealing, and they may be into extreme sports.

The introverted sensation type

With this type it is the internal, subjectively experienced sensation that is important. Objects do not count much. They are so full of their own sensations that they may appear out of touch and find it hard to express themselves to others. This is because they are reacting subjectively to external events: they may even claim to see ghosts, visions and startling imagery. In extreme cases this type becomes psychotic and is unable to distinguish reality from fantasy. The shadow type is the extroverted intuitive type – this repressed function may lead to negative hunches about things that might be going to happen and even to paranoia. Some artists, musicians and writers may belong to this group, and Emma Jung placed herself in this category.

The extroverted intuitive type

This type uses the intuitive part of the brain whenever a judgement or decision has to be made without knowing the full facts. They like to look at a problem from all angles and see different points of view. They get bored with fixed, familiar, well-established things and like to explore the new and look to the future. Because of this they may view customs and convention as unimportant and may trample on other people in order to get what they want. They are 'chancers', with their own form of morality. They rarely see a thing through and their personal relationships are often weak. The shadow type is the introverted sensation type – the repressed function may lead them to compulsively addictive behaviour, phobias or hypochondria. Entrepreneurs, journalists, fashion designers and businessmen may belong to this group.

The introverted intuitive type

To this type, the mystical world of dreams, visions and the collective unconscious is important. They are often preoccupied with inner day-dreams, fantasies and religious revelations, and try to interpret the outer world in terms of these. In the past this type of person would probably have been the shaman of the tribe, but nowadays they are often rather outcast and regarded as being odd. The shadow type is the extroverted sensation type – as with the extroverted intuitive type, the repressed function may appear as compulsive behaviour, obsessions and hypochondria. These people are always in danger of losing touch with reality and may even become schizophrenic. Many psychics, mystics and poets belong in this group.

The idea of looking at the human psyche in terms of differing psychological types is still popular. After Jung's work was published, Isabel Briggs Myers and her mother took the idea further, and in 1942 they published the first version of a personality test called the Myers-Briggs Type Indicator that is still used today in various different forms.

What determines the psychological type

Jung argues that the inclination towards a dominant psychological type is basically inborn in the individual, basing this argument on the fact that two children of the same mother often display very different behaviour without any apparent difference in the attitude of the mother towards them. A person's psychological type begins to become apparent quite early in childhood. Its further development is then determined by a number of different factors:

- **Heredity** – genetic factors will tend to predispose a child to being more introverted or extroverted.
- **Parental type** – the child may identify with one or other parent and so begin to copy their behaviour. Alternatively, they may deliberately develop an opposite type in order to rebel.
- **Social factors** – whichever behaviour is encouraged and achieves the best results will also influence the development of a psychological type.

The family, school, peer group and so on are all important in reinforcing a child's personality type. Extrovert children soon appear to be more active, talkative, sociable and interested in their surroundings. They play freely and without fear. This type of outlook is favoured in modern Western society and so is often encouraged by parents and teachers, because they tend to see such a child as bright and outgoing. The introverted child, on the other hand, is shy and sometimes fearful, approaching objects and other people with caution and preferring to play alone. These children may cause anxiety among parents and teachers, but they are often creative and reflective, with rich imaginations.

Problems often arise when parents try to force a child into a mould that goes against the natural type. This sort of pressure can result in neurosis and hampers development in later life. If the parents are more flexible they can help the child towards developing its natural type. Often the unconscious function is projected onto others as the child grows – perhaps onto parents, siblings, peer group members, actors or pop stars. The child will identify with groups or fall in love with people who satisfy this function. Through a process of repeated projection and subsequent withdrawal, the whole psyche gradually becomes more integrated. This is why attachments of this sort are so important to the developing psyche.

Emotional involvement frequently occurs between patient and analyst during the course of therapy. This process is actually a kind of projection and is called **transference**. It can work in either direction and may be positive or negative in nature. It can be useful if it is handled sensitively, because once the feelings are being projected onto the other person it becomes possible to draw them out and look at them in the light of day. On the journey towards individuation the psyche is ever growing and changing. Jung's theory about the complementary pairs of opposites that make up the human personality can be useful in helping a person to see more clearly which energies are not in balance.

Forming relationships

It is of course rare, if not impossible, to find a person who represents a pure type. The types are really intended to represent general behavioural tendencies, rather than concrete personality categories. Most people are a mixture of at least two types, and more complex personalities probably incorporate more. Gaining insight into a person's psychological type can assist progress in therapy or help to understand a relationship. People may gradually change their type as they develop and mature. Integration of the different types within the personality can be seen as the goal of the individuation process. The more mature the psyche becomes, the more a person is consciously aware of different aspects of the Self.

People are often attracted to their opposite type because their partner expresses the neglected function. There are two dangers here:

- people may avoid achieving their own psychological wholeness because they see their neglected function as belonging to the other person

- because opposite types don't understand each other, many misunderstandings can arise.

When a person projects their own hidden aspect onto someone else, they 'fall in love' with them. As they become more aware of their own unconscious aspect, this projection tends to be withdrawn and they fall out of love again. Some people repeatedly go through this process over and over again without ever realizing why.

Sometimes people fall for the same type as themselves. This means that the dominant function tends to get over-emphasized and the suppressed one causes all sorts of havoc in the relationship. For example, two introverted intuitive poets might get together and live in a little fantasy world, totally neglecting their surroundings and living in squalor.

Two introverted intuitive poets living together.

Summary

- Jung identified two opposite and balanced attitudes – introversion and extroversion – which characterize human psychological make-up.
- He then established four different functions – thinking, feeling, sensation and intuition – which he grouped into two opposite and balanced pairs.
- The two attitudes and the four functions were then combined to produce eight different psychological types.
- A person's psychological type will influence their relationships and the way they function in the world. Most people are a mixture of two or more types.
- A person's psychological type can change and mature throughout their life. More integrated people are more consciously aware of all the different functions within their personality.

08

the esoteric and the paranormal

In this chapter you will learn:
- the background to Jung's studies of Gnosticism and alchemy
- how the *I-Ching* led Jung to new ideas about how the psyche works
- about Jung's long-standing interest in astrology.

Jung had a huge diversity of interests and he worked very much outside the mainstream thinking of his day. He did not see human beings as purely biological organisms in the way that Freud had attempted to, nor was he interested only in treating neurosis and mental illness as some psychiatrists were. For him, the spiritual aspects of the psyche were both fascinating and vitally important. In fact, he saw the numinous aspects of human psychology as holding the true key to therapy.

Throughout his long life Jung had a fascination with exploring the esoteric and the paranormal and he wrote an enormous amount about subjects relating to both areas. His range of interest was vast and this approach was quite deliberate, because he was searching for universal truths within human psychology that would link up with his theories about the collective unconscious. He was almost certainly a genius, but people who react in a negative way to his work vary between those who see him as a sort of self-styled guru or mystic and those who slate him as a charlatan. His interest in the occult has made him open to the latter criticism and his ideas have been widely misunderstood.

Gnosticism

Gnosticism is a religious and philosophical movement, which probably originated around the fourth century BC. There were many different Gnostic sects, all concerned with knowledge of the occult and magical. *Gnosis* is derived from a Greek word, meaning 'knowledge'.

Jung studied Gnosticism in depth from about 1918 until 1926. His interest arose in the first place because he was very keen to establish historical and literary links with his ideas about human psychology. He saw his analytical psychology as being fundamentally a natural science, but he was well aware that it was all too easy to introduce personal bias to his findings. He needed some kind of credibility and he thought that this might be achieved if he could demonstrate parallels between his own thinking and that of the Gnostics. In the writings of the Gnostics he saw an uninterrupted intellectual chain that could give substance to his own ideas.

Jung discovered that mythological ideas within Gnosticism had great relevance to his ideas about the human psyche. It seemed to him that the Gnostics had been confronted with the archetypal world of the unconscious and had tried to understand its contents just as he had. In Gnostic thinking, nature and creation are fundamentally flawed and separated from the original true god. The world is ruled over by its creator, who is not really the original god, but a sort of 'half-god' or 'demi-urge'. He is assisted by seven beings called 'archons', who try to enslave people and prevent their return to the original divine realm. Gnosis was supposed to offer a key to the return to the divine.

Jung saw this myth as being symbolic of the individuation process, where the soul goes on an inner spiritual quest, seeking inner unity with the Self. At the start of the quest it is as blind to its true nature as the Gnostic soul is to the nature of the true god. Jung was excited about this because it seemed to show that his ideas were not new and had indeed been at large throughout history. Eventually, however, he decided that Gnostic teachings were too remote and obscure to be very helpful – they had been formulated a very long time ago and the fragmented knowledge we have of them was mainly recorded by Christians, who were in fact rivals to the Gnostics. Jung needed something else to give weight to his theories and he stumbled upon the very thing when he began to study alchemy.

Alchemy

Alchemy is an esoteric practice combining aspects of mysticism, magic, science and religion. In many ways it was the forerunner of modern chemistry, as well as many of our concepts about the psychology of the unconscious. When Jung first began reading about it he found it rather far-fetched and difficult to understand. However, in 1928 an oriental scholar called Richard Wilhelm sent him *The Secret of the Golden Flower*, which was a medieval manuscript of yoga and alchemy; Wilhelm asked Jung to write a psychological commentary on it. As we have already seen in Chapter 03, this book linked up with Jung's own dreams, and he soon realized that it gave him exciting confirmation of his own ideas. He became seriously interested in alchemy and was eventually to be profoundly affected by its insights: studying alchemical manuscripts from the sixteenth and seventeenth centuries was to absorb him for the next decade.

Alchemy was very popular during medieval times, and was practised until the end of the seventeenth century and beyond, but its roots stretch back much further into history, at least as far as ancient Egypt. The best-known aspect of alchemy is the idea of trying to turn base metals into gold, but in fact there was a lot more to it than that. The ultimate goal was an inner transformation of the alchemist's psyche, and it was this aspect that interested Jung the most. He saw alchemy as bridging the frustrating gap between ancient Gnosticism and modern sciences such as chemistry and the psychology of the unconscious. Alchemical thought coincided in surprising ways with his own ideas about the unconscious – it looked at the problem of matter, as well as the union of opposites such as male and female, God and man. It was also interested in attempting to balance thinking by including the feminine principle – a consideration which interested Jung especially in connection with matters of religion (for more about this see Chapter 09). Because of these parallels, Jung saw alchemy as the historical counterpart of his analytical psychology that he had been looking for. This gave more substance and credibility to his ideas.

Alchemy is full of weird fantasy images, which Jung soon realized were archetypal in nature. This was important because he realized that understanding historical ideas could be vital in understanding the psychology of the unconscious. The idea of turning base metal into gold was rooted in still earlier ideas about the four elements – earth, air, fire and water. Every physical form was supposed to contain these four elements in different proportions. Alchemists believed that if one could somehow alter the balance between the elements, then one could turn base metal into gold, or indeed any substance into any other substance. Success depended very much upon the alchemist's state of mind, which naturally had to be pure, so prayer and meditation were part of the practice.

Jung was intrigued to find alchemical imagery cropping up in the dreams of patients who were going through the individuation process. He studied the alchemical process and found that it went through a series of stages, each one of which could also represent a stage in the development of the maturing psyche:

- **Nigredo or 'blackness'**. This is the first stage, where the alchemist heats material up until it goes black. This represents the first stage of individuation, where the person begins to break down the barriers between conscious and unconscious. This stage is often accompanied by depression –

The alchemist's state of mind naturally had to be pure.

the 'dark night of the soul' or 'Nekyia' (night-sea journey), as the person begins to face the inner darkness of the shadow.

- **Albedo or 'whiteness'.** This is the next stage, when white flecks appear in the mixture, which eventually crystallizes as a white stone. This represents the gradual cleansing of the psyche as the inner darkness is faced. People often confront and converse with archetypes at this stage, and interestingly the alchemists reported meeting all kinds of frightening archetypal beings wandering around their labs.

- **Rubedo or 'redness'.** This is the final stage, when mercury is added to the white stone, which goes green, then red. This process represents the union of opposites and the result – called *elixir vitae* (the elixir of life) – can bring long life or even immortality. It is represented symbolically by a winged hermaphrodite figure or a rose. This stage represents the final stage of analysis – the resolution of psychic conflicts and the balancing of opposites. Jung remarked that much of his work was concerned with this type of balancing process.

Through studying alchemy, Jung came to realize that the unconscious is not a thing, or a place, but a process. The psyche is transformed and developed by the relationship of the ego to the contents of the unconscious. We can see this process reflected in the individual through dreams and fantasies; in the collective mind it shows in religious systems and their symbols, and also in myths. It was through studying these processes and symbols that Jung arrived at the central concept of his psychology – the process of individuation.

The *I-Ching*

Jung's early interest in omens and paranormal occurrences led him towards an exploration of various types of **divination**. He developed a special interest in the *I-Ching*, which is an ancient Chinese method of divination. The *I-Ching* is also known as the *Book of Changes* and this gives a clue to the philosophy behind it. From ancient times the Chinese have seen the whole of creation as being made up of intertwined male and female energies, each carrying the seed of the other. This is represented by the well-known black and white yin and yang symbol.

The universe is in a constant state of change as the two primal forces flow in and out of each other. This idea of wholeness and the balancing of two opposite forces fits in very well with Jung's ideas, and the yin and yang symbol is another example of the archetypal mandala. To consult the *I-Ching*, yarrow stalks or coins were usually used. Short and long stalks, or the two sides of a coin, represented the two primal forces. The stalks or coins were thrown and the random patterns they made were then

The yin and yang symbol.

interpreted using a special book of wise sayings. Jung, in the peace of his retreat at Bollingen, used reeds in place of yarrow stalks.

Jung was fascinated by the results he obtained from *I-Ching* readings. He found many meaningful connections with his own thought processes which he could not explain to himself. He began to use the *I-Ching* with his patients too, and found that a significant number of the answers given were relevant to the patients' problems. For example, a young client was wondering whether he should marry a certain girl; when the *I-Ching* was consulted it gave the reply: 'The maiden is powerful. One should not marry such a maiden.' The girl seemed suitable, but deep down the young man was afraid that she would soon become like his dominating mother.

Jung began to wonder how such meaningful answers could emerge from the *I-Ching*. How did the connection between the inner, psychic event and the outer, physical event come about? Jung suggested the idea of 'acausal parallelism', by which he meant that everything that happens is related to everything else, and everything is actually happening at the same time. He felt that there was an acausal archetypal order of this kind at the root of all phenomena. Thus, two events could be connected in some way without one necessarily having to be the direct cause of the other. He later used the word 'synchronicity' to express this idea.

Synchronicity

Science has tended to train people to think that A causes B which causes C, in a neat, orderly, linear fashion – so related events are connected by cause and effect. This idea is known as **causality**. Eastern thinking, as Jung discovered by playing with the *I-Ching*, has long taught that there is another way in which events can be connected: A and B are connected, but neither need be the cause of the other. This is what Jung called synchronicity and he suggested that coincidences worked in this way.

Jung wondered if a law of synchronicity could be established, contrasting with the law of causality. He was very excited by the idea of discovering a place where psychology and physics could meet. The renowned physicist Albert Einstein (1879–1955) was several times a guest of Jung's at dinner, and he attempted to explain his theories of relativity to the non-physicists present.

This started Jung thinking that there could perhaps be relativity of time as well as space, and this led eventually to his ideas about synchronicity.

Jung's ideas were very unusual and he waited many years before putting them forward publicly. Eventually he discovered that some scientists, notably physicist Wolfgang Pauli (1900–58, Nobel Laureate in Physics 1945), were interested in his ideas. He finally published his findings in tandem with Pauli in a collection of essays called *The Interpretation of Nature and the Psyche*. Modern quantum physics seems happy to accept acausal effects in its physical theories. Physicists have even suggested that physical bodies can sometimes have an effect upon one another without any apparent exchange of energy taking place between them. The universe seems to consist no longer of facts, but of possibilities.

Jung was especially interested in the more startling coincidences, those that seemed to be so meaningful that it was virtually impossible for them to have occurred by chance alone.

For example, he was listening one day to a young woman patient who was relating to him a dream about being given a golden scarab. As she spoke he heard a tapping on the window, and upon opening it he found a scarabaeid beetle, the local equivalent of the golden scarab. The woman was so surprised by this event that it changed her whole way of thinking, breaking down her rational defences and leading to new mental maturity. The scarab, as Jung pointed out, is an archetypal symbol of rebirth.

Simple coincidences, such as reading a new word in the paper and then immediately coming across it in the crossword, did not hold quite such fascination for Jung.

Such archetypal symbolism often seems to crop up in connection with synchronous events. In *Memories, Dreams, Reflections,* Jung gives a startlingly vivid example of this when he describes an event that took place one night at Bollingen in the late winter or early spring of 1923–4. It was a very still night, but he was disturbed by weird dreams: first of all he felt that someone was prowling around the tower, and then later on he dreamed that a long procession of hundreds of young men was coming down from the mountains and pouring around the tower, trampling, shouting, singing and playing music. On both occasions he was puzzled to look outside and find that there was nobody there and the night was as still as before: he describes the dreams as being so real that it felt much more like an experience of haunting.

It was much later that he stumbled upon an account in a seventeenth-century chronicle which described a very similar experience: a man climbing in the local mountains was disturbed one night by a procession of men pouring past his hut, playing music and singing. In the morning a local herdsman told him that Wotan's army of departed souls was in the habit of appearing in this way.

Jung felt that it was not enough to describe his own experience as a mere dream or hallucination. He felt that it had to be real in some strange way, especially in the light of the seventeenth-century account, and suggests that it was in fact a synchronistic phenomenon. Such phenomena often prove to have some correspondence in external reality. Jung later discovered that there was indeed a real parallel to his experience in the outer world, when such gatherings actually took place in the Middle Ages. Local young men would gather together, usually in spring, to celebrate and bid their homeland farewell before marching off to serve as soldiers in foreign lands.

Astrology

Jung was interested in astrology because it, too, tied in with his ideas about archetypes and the collective unconscious. He did a great deal of careful research, and by 1911 he had learned how to draw up natal charts and studied how they linked up with events in people's lives. He was fascinated by the idea that a person's private world could be affected by far-reaching aspects of cosmic activity. However, he was not at all interested in the generalized type of astrology that appears in newspapers and magazines, and he was not convinced that people are much influenced by their sun sign. He was more interested in the season in which a person was born, and the effects that the planets could have on the personality.

Jung decided that astrology would be a good way of conducting experiments to show synchronicity at work as a natural law in its own right. He studied the birth charts of married couples, to see if the positions of the planets in the two natal charts tied in with the actual marriage event. If this could be shown to happen, then he would have established a meaningful acausal link. He did not find a direct correlation, but what he did find was equally fascinating – he found that the results of analysis varied according to who was doing the analysis. In other words, a person's subjective expectations were somehow mirrored in the results. Modern quantum physics is beginning to see this as a real possibility – the observer can affect the results of an experiment simply by the act of observing.

Jung was also interested in the 'precession of the equinoxes'. This phrase refers to the fact that the astrological sign in which the spring equinox occurs moves slowly backwards through one degree of longitude every 72 years. So every 2000 years the sign on the horizon at the time of equinox changes. At the moment we are just leaving the Age of Pisces and entering the Age of Aquarius. Jung believed that this phenomenon had far-reaching effects upon both historical events and human spirituality. Each 2000-year change heralds the beginning of a new spiritual trend. Interestingly, Jesus was born at the beginning of the Age of Pisces, and his sign is often shown as that of the fish. We are now apparently due for a change as we enter the Age of Aquarius.

Astrology was not considered to be a subject for serious study in Jung's day. In fact, it was very much frowned upon as a superstitious practice: many of his followers and students have seen his interest as a great source of embarrassment and tried to gloss over it. The *Freud/Jung Letters* show that he tried to get backing from Freud for his interest, saying that he considered astrology to be essential to a proper understanding of mythology. Initially Freud encouraged his interest, but cautioned him that he would be accused of mysticism, and should not dwell too long on astrological studies. Jung was undeterred and in a subsequent letter to Freud he said that he was hoping to discover much archetypal knowledge in astrology, particularly in connection with the signs of the zodiac. Once again Freud replied with encouragement, but also another caution, warning Jung to be careful about publishing his ideas. After their break-up in 1913 Freud became openly critical of Jung's excursions into the paranormal.

Jung never lost his interest in astrology, and if he was working with a particularly difficult case he sometimes had the person's birth chart cast in order to gain greater understanding. In 1947 he wrote a letter to Hindu astrologer B. V. Raman, in which he explained that astrological data often shed light on aspects of a person's personality that would otherwise have been very hard to understand. His opinion was that astrology was interesting to the psychologist because projected psychological experiences were evident in the constellations. Although Jung never lost his interest in astrology, he eventually concentrated more upon alchemy in his writing and public speaking. This was probably safer, because nobody was paying much attention to alchemy at the time, so it did not have the same stigma attached to it as astrology had, although alchemical writing actually contains a great deal of astrological material and is full of archetypal symbolism.

As above so below

Jung's view of the human psyche in many ways reflected the ancient occult maxim 'as above so below'. For him, events in the outer world of material things were often reflected in the inner world of the psyche. He found this idea reflected in his studies of astrology and alchemy. The effect could also take place in reverse, with the individual affecting the surroundings, for example in the case of the loud bangs in the bookcase when Jung was talking to Freud about the paranormal. Jung discovered that as patients got deeper into therapy, synchronous psychic events became more frequent in their lives. These often seemed to occur in connection with strong emotions, and Jung suggested that as the threshold of conscious control is lowered, so the unconscious and its contents begin to show themselves in the outer world. He concluded that a human being is not an isolated little psyche, but part of a vast network of interacting energy that can affect us in many unexpected ways. Since psyche and matter are part of the same unfathomable universe and in constant contact with each other, Jung thought it possible, if not probable, that they actually represented two different aspects of a whole.

Jung felt that a lot of personal psychological problems arose from a sort of family or cultural karma – problems that had not been resolved by one's forebears were passed on to be sorted out by the next generation. He said that many problems are more to do with the social environment than the individual and are therefore linked to the collective unconscious. Jung observed that so far psychological therapy has been slow to take this into account.

Jung's view of the world was often subjective, concentrating on the inner world of dreams, visions and synchronous events. He saw his life's quest as being one of achieving understanding of his own unconscious and so, in many ways, the inner world was even more important to him than the outer world. At times he would deliberately try to shut himself off from the sensory input of the outside world and spend time alone in order to enter his own rich, inner world. If we live too much in the outer world, he said, we become too much involved in the present, and gain little understanding of the ways in which our unconscious, ancestral psyches are listening and responding. It is essential to listen to voice of the unconscious in order to balance the historical psychological aspects of our being with the ever-changing conditions of the present.

Jung explained that in our ordinary everyday minds we are caught in the worlds of time and space. Beyond that, when we are in touch with the archetypes and the collective unconscious, we enter a world where the normal rules of space and time are no longer relevant. Through his studies of the esoteric and the paranormal, in the peace and silence of his retreat at Bollingen, Jung was able to achieve this state of being and 'see life in the round'. But he stressed that he was sailing here into uncharted waters, and there was much to be discovered by those who followed after him. He said that he could not enter what he called the 'four-dimensional system' at will – it could only happen *to* him. It was therefore not an experience that was easily open to scientific experiment. Modern psychology is still struggling with this kind of difficulty.

Summary

- Jung was fascinated by a wide range of esoteric and paranormal studies.
- In these studies he was searching for universal truths within human psychology that would link up with his theories about the collective unconscious.
- In both Gnosticism and alchemy he discovered archetypal symbolism and mythology that supported his theories.
- His studies of divination and astrology led him to suggest the existence of a second natural law, that of 'synchronicity', which worked alongside the law of causality.
- Jung believed that events in the outer world of material things were often reflected in the inner world of the psyche, and vice versa.

09

religion and spirituality

In this chapter you will learn:
- more about Jung's spiritual attitude
- the basics of what he had to say about the problem of evil
- how he turned to the East to gain greater understanding of religious psychology.

Jung's spiritual attitude

Jung was by nature a spiritually aware person – in fact, this was one of the most important aspects of his life. However, he had a tendency to attack the dogma of the great religious faiths, asserting that only spontaneous, personal religious experiences led to real spiritual truth. In religious matters, as in psychotherapy, it was the individual's unique life experience that really counted in Jung's view. He maintained that the unconscious is the only source of our spiritual experience and that the individual can only attain enlightenment through a process of painstaking self-examination. Jung always tried to approach religious questions from the point of view of a rational scientist, and he explored many different religious angles in his search for universal truths.

Jung used biblical references quite frequently in his writing and also made references to the Apocrypha. This is a collection of texts that is included in some versions of the Bible as 'inter-testamental' material – meaning that they come after the latest books of the Old Testament and before the books of the New Testament. As was the case with his studies of Gnosticism and alchemy, Jung used these texts as a source of material to support his own analytical psychology. Once again he emphasized the symbolic and mythological aspects, which gave archetypal insights and were used to express ideas that could not be expressed directly in ordinary language.

Although Jung was always drawn to discover more about the numinous, his relationship with Christianity was always somewhat ambiguous. He found the conservative dogma and ritual of his father's type of Christianity too limiting. In fact, he found some of the ideas involved positively distasteful – above all, the idea that God, who had made people imperfect in the first place, could be appeased by the sacrifice of his own son. As he attempted to grow away from his religious upbringing he developed some ambivalent attitudes. Meanwhile, his mother's views were less rigid and she introduced him to ideas from other religions and encouraged his early interest in the paranormal.

During a BBC radio broadcast in 1959, John Freeman asked Jung if he believed in God. His famous reply, 'I don't need to believe … I know', led to more controversy for Jung. He later explained that he had been put on the spot and had uttered the first words that came into his head. What he had meant to convey was that he was aware of the existence of archetypal

God-images, and also of his own experience of what is commonly referred to as God. This experience was an experience of a greater will, over and above that of his individual consciousness. He found that it often put strange ideas into his head, and sometimes prompted him to move in directions that seemed beyond his conscious knowledge or comprehension. Jung said that this archetypal pattern of God existed in all people, and contained all the energies for transformation and individuation in the individual.

Jung claimed that all his thoughts ultimately revolved around God and that he felt it would be very wrong to ignore the importance of this. Although he considered the religious aspects of his work to be vitally important, he never wanted to dictate to other people what they should believe, or indeed appear to be superior in any way. He regarded himself as simply a tool of God – a 'spoon in his kitchen' – trying to guide people in their individuation process. At the same time he always retained a small but fierce element of personal pride. God, he explained, needs man in order to illuminate his creation. This attitude, which Jung retained all his life, went right back to the game he played as a small boy sitting on his stone and asking himself, 'Am I the one who is sitting on the stone, or am I the stone on which he is sitting?'

The problem of evil

Astrological ideas suggested to Jung that the Age of Pisces had coincided with the birth of Christ and the subsequent growth of Christianity. Jung emphasized that for him the Christian insistence that God the Father and Jesus were sinless beings represented an unbalanced attitude – a total denial of the shadow. Jung predicted an eventual inevitable swing to counteract this trend. He saw this beginning with the nineteenth-century teachings of thinkers such as Marx and Darwin, whose rationalist, materialist stance came into conflict with Christianity. But Jung felt that modern man had gained scientific insight at the cost of losing his soul – he is no longer in contact with the numinous.

A lack of understanding of what goes on in the unconscious is dangerous because it means that we are afraid to confront the shadow and therefore do not develop the capacity to deal with evil. Jung asserts that none of us is without our darker aspects. It is important in religious matters, as in human relationships, to see and acknowledge our imperfections because, 'where love stops, power begins, and violence and terror'. Chilling words.

Jung's attitude to the problem of evil is probably the most important way in which his thinking differs from traditional Christian theology. He struggled during his teens with a great spiritual crisis that led him to the idea that God must have a darker side to his nature, otherwise he would never have created the serpent in order to tempt Adam and Eve towards sin. In other words, God must have made the first people with a deliberate capacity for sin.

Jung's teenage vision of God shattering the whole of his cathedral with an enormous turd was followed by an indescribable sense of relief – he realized that what really mattered for him was to follow the will of the living, active God, rather than blindly following handed-down traditions and Biblical texts. From this experience also came the 'dim understanding that God could be something terrible'. For Jung, in fact, God was both 'the annihilating fire and an indescribable grace'. Once again we find the idea of balanced opposites that is so important in Jung's thinking.

Jung struggled with these ideas all his life and in 1951, when he was 76 and recuperating from a grave illness from which he thought he would never recover, he published an interesting little book called *Aion*. This book put forward controversial answers to the questions that had troubled him for many years about the dark side of God's nature. He felt that the book seemed to write itself and he had little control over it, but it enabled him to express ideas that he had long kept secret. The book explores the archetype of the God-image, exploring the ways in which it has evolved over the years, and showing how it is reflected in symbolic imagery in dreams, myths and art. Its main theme is the change in psychic consciousness that is occurring as we leave the Age of Pisces and enter the Age of Aquarius. Pisces – the fish that *live in* water – is a symbol that can represent the psyche. Aquarius, on the other hand, is the *carrier of* the water and so lives outside it. The new aeon cycle therefore represents a change from being controlled to being the controller. This means that the psyche will no longer be controlled by religious communities, but will instead be carried by spiritually conscious individuals.

Needless to say, Jung's message in *Aion* has still been largely ignored. Shortly after its publication Jung published another highly controversial book called *Answer to Job*. This book had been foreshadowed by a long dream in which he found himself kneeling before God, but could not bring himself to put his forehead totally to the floor – there was about a millimetre to spare. This tiny vestige of defiance represented man's mental reservations even in the face of divine decrees. Such reservations are what gives man his freedom and allows him to challenge the creator.

The story of Job

Answer to Job was published in 1952, towards the end of Jung's life. As with *Aion,* Jung needed a lot of courage to write the book and he realized that it would unleash a fresh storm of criticism. In *Answer to Job* Jung uses his own interpretation of the Old Testament story of Job to explore his idea of the shadow aspect of God. The story tells of how the devil bets God that Job, an honest and upright man, will turn against him if he is tormented enough. God takes the devil up on this and sends Job all kinds of nasty trials and tribulations. Jung's fundamental question is this: if God is all-good, and all-encompassing, then where does evil come from, and how does God permit it to exist? Jung suggests that the Old Testament God who torments Job is unpleasant and frightening and yet demands love from Job. For Jung this is a demonstration of God's shadow side. Job eventually survives his ordeals by seeking God's help against God, and so the story expresses God's dual nature as both tormentor and redeemer. Jung argues from this that good and evil are two halves of a great paradoxical whole. All that we call good is always balanced by an equally substantial evil. Evil cannot be argued to have come from man, because 'The Evil One' existed before man as one of the 'Sons of God' (Satan was originally one of God's angels).

Jung's idea is that God actually goes through an individuation process of his own, gradually becoming more mature and whole. He traces the course of this development through the Bible until we reach the point where God really wants to transform himself through becoming human. Eventually, by being incarnated as Jesus, God fully experiences what he had made Job suffer.

Jung was fascinated by the weird apocalyptic visions in the Book of Revelation at the end of the Bible. He suggests that they represent a final confrontation with the shadow, where God gives vent to his anger at the way his creation has turned out.

Jung suggests that after the apocalypse a new divine Goddess figure will emerge, representing a balancing energy after an era of male dominance and destructiveness. What Jung really seems to be suggesting is the idea that as people's understanding of God evolves, so God himself (or herself?) also evolves.

The notion that God could have a negative shadow side has perturbed a lot of Christians, and many critics have been extremely hostile. But in his answers to furious theologians Jung emphasised that he was speaking about the God-image – the idea or representation that man makes of God – rather than God himself, who is mysterious and unfathomable. The problem arose, he said, because people fail to see that the concepts of 'good' and 'evil' are actually moral judgements, and have nothing to do with the incomprehensible nature of 'Being', which is God himself. The basic idea behind *Answer to Job* is really that we all need to transform the negativity in ourselves before we can hope to transform the outer world. The paradoxical God image forces us to confront our own shadow. This is what we are trying to do in the search for the Self. The Self represents a deeper, wiser aspect of our being that knows our life's purpose and our true path.

The journey towards the Self

Jung saw Christ as providing people with an archetypal image of the Self that they can aspire to. Other religions have their own figures, such as Buddha, who also represent spiritual perfection and wholeness. Just as God sent his son Christ into the world, so each of us sends our ego into the outer world. The goal of the individuation process is the eventual re-integration of the ego, whereupon it ceases to occupy centre stage in our consciousness. This is a lengthy and very painful process, which Jung compares with the difficult initiation tests often undergone by members of shamanic tribes. Such tests are often designed to bring initiates to the brink of death, after which they emerge with new spiritual awareness. The shaman can then become a healer and spiritual teacher.

Jung identifies this archetypal death and rebirth process occurring in different forms in many cultures and religious traditions, for example in:

• the death and resurrection of Jesus

- the alchemical process where a base metal is broken down and eventually transmuted into the *elixir vitae*
- shamanic initiation rituals
- ancient Egyptian myths, where again the god dies and is reborn.

Interestingly, in the Egyptian tradition rebirth was originally only a possibility for the Pharaoh, who was a god-like being, but eventually it was available to others who followed the correct burial rites. Jung's vision was that eventually a kind of psychic rebirth would be available for everyone who was willing to undergo the individuation process.

Naturally Jung's unorthodox views about religion opened him to criticism from theologians, who resented his trespassing on their territory. He disagreed totally with fundamentalist points of view, where people held that their own particular brand of belief represented absolute truth. Jung tended more towards the Gnostic view that it was knowledge that counted, rather than faith. He cautioned that whenever dogma takes over human minds, they lose sight of whatever spiritual insights they had in the first place.

For Jung, the divine manifests within each individual in a different way, and through exploring personal symbols in dreams and fantasies he helped his patients to come to their own understanding. This intensely personal experience of the divine is what Jung described as the 'numinosum'. The experience feels as if it comes from outside the individual and cannot be brought on by an effort of will. Experience of the numinosum is the key to healing and it always carries a feeling of awakening and being connected to something beyond oneself. It may be connected with an ordinary, everyday experience; usually it is related in some way to the person's area of greatest weakness and it always manifests for the purpose of healing. Sometimes it appears in a very unorthodox, even frightening form, for example a person may develop a fascination with death, or with some sort of erotic symbol. This can make it difficult to recognize the numinosum when it appears. Whenever it does appear it is experienced as a powerful compelling force that is somehow endowed with great significance to the individual. Because the numinosum is connected to our woundedness and weakness, it is very important in analysis to explore and try to understand the shadow – knowledge of the shadow may lead us to the numinosum and vice versa.

Hinduism

Jung felt it was necessary for him as a psychologist to explore comparative religion in as much depth as possible, so he also made in-depth studies of some of the Eastern religions. In the Hindu faith there are lots of gods and goddesses, who all originate from an original creative force called Brahma. Each god or goddess symbolically represents a different divine aspect – such as Vishnu, the creator, Shiva the destroyer, or Krishna the god of love. Unlike in the Christian tradition, the shadow side of the divine is openly portrayed. In 1937 Jung visited India and found himself mainly interested in the question of the psychological nature of evil (for more about his visit to India see Chapter 10).

Jung also became interested in Yoga, which is a Hindu system of philosophy using physical exercises, breathing and meditation as a means to attaining ultimate reunion with the divine. He found the physical postures helpful for calming the mind and he was fascinated by the symbolic process of spiritual transformation described in the Yogic texts. Once again he found a description of the archetypal process of separation and eventual rebalancing of opposites, just as he had seen it in alchemical texts. Jung saw the physical and meditative processes of Yoga as a useful means of relaxing the ego's grip over the unconscious, so that the individuation process could get underway. But he cautioned Western people not to go too deeply into the more obscure practises of Yoga, warning that Western minds are not usually properly prepared and that psychosis could result.

Although he was impressed by the Hindu religion and Yoga, Jung could not accept the ultimate goal, which is a bliss state involving the total absorption of the Self into the divine. He argued that such a state would be logically impossible, because if there is no Self, then there is no consciousness, so who can be experiencing the bliss state? In any case, he was not at all happy with an ultimate goal that seemed to represent a total escape from reality. This seemed to him to be pointless and he believed instead that each of us is in the world for a special purpose, which is known to the Self and which it is our task to discover. The goal of Jungian analysis was to help people towards wholeness and to function more fully in the real world. For this reason Jung did not wish to be freed from other human beings, nor from himself, or from nature, because all these appeared to him to be 'the greatest of miracles'. To withdraw before he had achieved all that he was able to do in the world felt to him like amputating part of his psyche. He further cautioned that whatever we deliberately leave behind and forget has a habit of returning to us with added force.

Buddhism

The goal of Buddhism is to attain an inner state of enlightenment, once again detaching oneself from the physical world and the endless chatter of the psyche. In Zen Buddhism the student studies riddles called *koans,* for example: 'What is the sound of one hand clapping?' Of course there is no logical answer – the purpose of the *koan* is to demonstrate the futility of trying to achieve enlightenment through logical thinking. Jung saw parallels here with psychological therapy, where the aim is to alter conscious awareness and so achieve a higher spiritual state.

Jung was particularly interested in *The Tibetan Book of the Dead* – a sort of travel guide for the departed soul. This tied up with other texts that he had discovered, for example in ancient Egyptian mythology, where there is also a *Book of the Dead*. He had explored similar themes when he wrote the *Septem Sermones* (1916) and once again he was struck by the archetypal nature of the teachings that he found cropping up in different cultures. In other Buddhist teachings he found more vivid archetypal imagery, such as the 'jewel in the crown of the lotus', which he saw as another mandala-like symbolic image of the Self.

Buddhism appealed to Jung because:

- it is up to each person to follow their own path to enlightenment – there is little emphasis upon dogma and faith
- the answer to spiritual growth is seen as lying within – there is no external deity as such
- the spiritual teachings and meditations are helpful for training the mind towards concentration.

Nevertheless, he also found that there were drawbacks. In Buddhism, suffering is seen as an illusion from which one can ultimately escape through attaining enlightenment. Jung disagreed, saying that suffering is real and unavoidable. We can only overcome suffering by living through it, and analytical psychology can help us to do that. Also, withdrawal from life is in itself a form of repression – a denial of the shadow – and as such would tend eventually to produce an opposite swing. Finally, in Buddhism there is an endless cycle of reincarnation, where the individual is born and dies and is born again. The only escape from this dismal trap is through enlightenment. Jung says that this is no good for the Western mind, which needs to feel that it progresses towards a goal and has a purpose to its existence.

After travelling extensively in the East, Jung was eventually drawn back to study Western teachings. He realized that the study of Eastern religions had been important to him, but that it was only a part of the path that would bring him to his goal. He compared the Eastern way of thinking with that of the West and concluded that:

- Western man is mainly extroverted, finding meaning in external objects and looking for meaning in the 'real world'. Consciousness in Western man is too detached from the unconscious.

- Eastern man is mainly introverted and looks for meaning within the Self. In Eastern man the tendency is for consciousness to merge completely with the unconscious.

'But,' said Jung, 'the meaning is both without and within.' He had discovered that both traditions had their own strengths and drawbacks. Neither point of view was completely right or completely wrong. This insight shows a move towards balance and maturity within Jung's own psyche – an integration of the two sides of his personality that had troubled him for so long.

Changes in Christian thinking

Jung came to believe that Christianity was of central importance to Western man, but it needed to gain new insights in order to answer the spiritual needs of modern people. For example, he felt that there was an imbalance in the doctrine of the Trinity, which sees God as having three aspects – Father, Son and Holy Spirit. Jung felt that this idea did not acknowledge a feminine aspect to the divine. Gnostic teaching had actually added a 'fourth term' as an attempt to incorporate the hidden and mysterious feminine side. The immense popular appeal of such recent books as Dan Brown's *The Da Vinci Code* shows that Jung was not far off the mark in his understanding that the modern mind tends to seek such a balance.

In 1950 the Catholic Church announced a new doctrine – that of the Assumption of the Virgin Mary. Jung considered this new dogma to be 'the most important religious event since the reformation' (*Answer to Job*). Before this, from early times, the Church had tended to regard the feminine with deep suspicion. The problem had begun with the doctrine of Original Sin, which says that we are all born sinful, ever since Adam and Eve ate the forbidden fruit. (Naughty temptress Eve was largely responsible for this.) But people began to realize that new-born babies can hardly have done anything sinful, so they decided that it must be the sexual act itself that causes all the trouble. The Virgin Mary was exempt from this indiscretion, having produced Jesus without having to have sex. In 1950 she gained a further promotion when the doctrine of the Assumption decreed that she was taken straight up to heaven, body and spirit, when she died and didn't have to wait for the Day of Judgement like the rest of us.

Jung saw this new doctrine as being very important because he felt that it acknowledged an archetypal psychological need. Ordinary people had always shown this need in the way that they regarded the Virgin as a comforting, motherly person, whom one could pray to in times of need. She had definitely been venerated all along, even though she wasn't 'officially' divine. People had visions of her too, and Jung points out that she often appeared to children. 'In such cases,' he said, 'the collective unconscious is always at work' (*Answer to Job*).

Jung's suggestion is that the doctrine of the Assumption is like a subconscious announcement that Mary is now being accepted as part of the Trinity, so that it becomes a 'Quaternity'. The doctrine 'expresses a renewed hope for the fulfilment of that yearning for peace which stirs deep down in the soul, and for a resolution of the threatening tension between opposites' (*Answer to Job*). Once again we have the idea of balance. Four is a more balanced number than three and Jung points out that it has often cropped up before – the four evangelists, four seasons, four elements and so on – making it a number that is archetypally satisfying. Just to be difficult, one could suggest that something is still missing from the divine group. If we have a father and a son then surely we need a daughter as well as a mother? Ought we not to have the number 5 to represent wholeness?

Jung believed that the study of religion was very important in giving us insight into the workings of the unconscious. He stressed that when he spoke of God he referred to the 'God within'. Whether or not God exists as a separate external entity was for Jung a pointless and unanswerable question, but he believed that it was essential for people to have a spiritual dimension in their lives and that numerous neuroses arose because people overlooked this aspect of their being, especially as they moved into the second half of life. People tend to focus on the narrower aspects of life such as work, marriage or success, but all the while they stay unhappy because they are restricting themselves spiritually. This is why Jung saw spirituality as being vitally important to the achievement of wholeness in the human psyche.

Summary

- Jung saw the spiritual aspects of human experience as being of vital importance to the health of the psyche.
- He studied a wide range of different religions in order to gain insight into archetypal patterns in religious thinking.
- Jung found dogmatic fundamentalist religions unhelpful because they lead to disagreement and spiritual stagnation. He emphasised the importance of individual experience in spiritual growth and psychic health.
- He believed that religions need to grow and evolve in order to answer the deep spiritual needs of ordinary people.

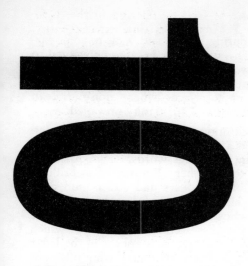

10

Jung the visionary

Travels

Jung travelled quite a lot during his life and went to some far-flung parts of the world. This was partly because he wanted to learn about cultures that were utterly different from his own in order to find out more about the collective unconscious. In order to do this he went to places where non-European languages and religions other than Christianity prevailed.

Jung visited North Africa more than once. In *Memories, Dreams, Reflections* there is a copy of a letter he sent to his wife Emma in 1920, beginning with the words, 'This Africa is incredible'. He goes on to give her glimpses of a brilliant morning in Algiers with bright houses and streets and dark clumps of tall palm trees. He then continued on by rail, a 30-hour stint to Tunis, whose classical Arab atmosphere mesmerized him until he was 'dissolved in the potpourri which cannot be evaluated'. Archetypal presences appear in the letter when he describes the rising sun as a 'great god' who 'fills both horizons with his joy and power'; he says that the moon at night 'glows with such divine clarity that one cannot doubt the existence of Astarte.' (Astarte is an ancient Semitic goddess whose widespread devotees included the Syrians, Phoenicians and Egyptians – in the Bible she is unkindly referred to as 'the abomination'.)

Jung saw so many interesting sights on the long train journey that although his descriptions are vivid, he says that he could not find enough words to describe everything properly to Emma. He was enthralled to stumble upon Roman remains everywhere, and see ancient amphorae for sale in the markets. 'I do not know what Africa is really saying to me,' he wrote, 'but it speaks.' And there were strangely synchronous events too – on arrival at Sousse with its white walls and towers he was astounded to see a sailing ship with two lateen sails that he had once painted. On another occasion, getting off a boat at Alexandria, Jung had his hand read by a chiromancer, who promptly announced that Jung was one of the very few great men he had seen and waived his normal fee.

Jung was struck by the way time seemed to slow down more and more the further he travelled into the Sahara, even threatening to move backwards. In a letter to a friend he described an encounter with a figure all swathed in white and seated upon a black mule whose harness was studded with silver. This man rode by without offering any greeting, but his proud bearing and the sense that this person was somehow wholly himself, struck Jung as a stark contrast to the average European with his 'faint note of foolishness' and his illusion of triumph in great achievements such as steamships and railways. He concluded that the driven attitude and suppression of emotion that characterizes modern Western culture have been gained at the expense of intensity of living. This has resulted in people forcing down into the unconscious much that is real and life-giving.

In 1924 Jung visited New Mexico, and here too this point was brought strongly home to him by Ochwiay Biano, a Pueblo Indian chief. This wise man graphically described the typical white man's face as being cruel and staring, as if they are always seeking something. His people, he added, did not understand what drove the white man in this way – they thought he was mad. When Jung asked him why this should be so, he replied that it was because they think 'with their heads'. Jung, surprised, asked him what he thought with himself, and the man indicated his heart – 'we think here,' he said. When Jung talked further with Ochwiay Biano, he discovered that his people had a strong belief that their religion was of benefit to the whole world, because they worshipped and encouraged the sun on its daily course across the sky. Jung concluded that this gave the people a sense that their lives were cosmologically meaningful: it was this deep sense of connectedness that had been lost by so-called civilized Western man.

Jung also visited Equatorial Africa where, in the primal stillness of the great plains which thronged with gigantic herds of many kinds of beasts, he had an important revelation. Here was a world that had always existed in such a way since time began, before there were any people to know that it was there. Seeing this, Jung suddenly grasped the cosmic meaning of consciousness – man was like a second creator. In observing the world and being consciously aware of it he gave it objective existence – and so man was indispensable for the completion of creation.

Shortly before the Second World War, in 1937, Jung was invited to visit India by the British Indian Government. This was to be the last of his great expeditions to study foreign culture. Some of his observations on Indian spirituality have already been discussed in Chapter 09. He realized that in India, as in many of the other cultures he had visited, people still lived in the whole body and had not retreated to live only from the head as they had in the West. On a visit to the Black Pagoda of Konarak, he observed that India still includes sexuality as an integral part of religion, quite unlike the way it has been totally banished in Western thinking. The entire pagoda is covered from top bottom with incredible obscene sculptures that were explained to Jung as being a means to achieve spiritual enlightenment. He questioned this, pointing out that the young men standing looking at the sculptures surely had nothing further from their minds. But that, apparently, was the whole point – they were there to remind people of spiritual laws and help them to clear the way to enlightenment by first fulfilling their karma. Jung advises anyone who is feeling morally superior to travel to Konarak, sit down in the shadow of the mighty ruin, and contemplate all their own reactions and feelings.

While he was in India, Jung had one of his 'big' dreams. He dreamed that he was looking at a castle on an island off the south coast of Britain, which he recognized as the home of the Holy Grail. He realized that it was his task to swim across alone to bring the grail home to this castle from an uninhabited solitary house on another small island. For Jung, this dream was a timely reminder that he needed to return to focus on his own people and culture. India was not his goal – it was simply a part of the road that was carrying him closer to his goal.

Jung and psychotherapy

Although Jung was such a great man he never claimed to be infallible as a therapist. He believed that about a third of his patients were really cured, another third considerably improved and the final third hardly affected by his efforts – although he acknowledged there was a problem in that beneficial effects might not show up until years later. Sometimes, if he felt that he was getting nowhere with a patient, he would refer them to a different type of analyst, acknowledging that no one approach represented the whole truth or would resonate with everybody. Where Freud believed that sexual repression was at the root of all neurosis, and Adler thought it was all about the struggle to achieve power, Jung believed that many people became neurotic because of a split in their psyche between the modern and the primitive. Deprived of the mythical truths of their ancestors, and cut off from the world of nature, they developed a huge gulf between the ego and the unconscious. In being helped to close this gulf a person can begin to achieve healing.

Jung always encouraged his patients to view him as a human being and he tried to establish very real relationships with them during their sessions, with a real sense of give and take. He never saw himself as a remote, clinical authority – he had realized while he was working at Burghölzli that unless the doctor got involved with the patient and allowed himself to be affected by their exchanges, he could not hope to help a person to heal. Jung always emphasized that only the wounded physician can heal, and even then only to the extent that he has managed to heal himself.

Unlike many other psychotherapists of his day, Jung sat face to face with his patients. This was quite unusual because many therapists followed Freud's methods, retaining a degree of anonymity and authority by sitting behind their patient, who reclined on a couch. Jung's was a more intimate approach and it helped his patients to see him as a human being, not just as a doctor. He did not carry this familiarity too far however – outside the consulting room he tended to be formal and polite, setting a little distance between himself and his client. He enjoyed helping people to explore their inner worlds, driven always by a sense of adventure and an insatiable curiosity, but he was not always interested in his clients' outpourings. On occasion his behaviour could be quite rude and dismissive – one woman who came to see him dissolved into copious tears during every session and he dealt with this by reading the newspaper!

Jung saw his role as being a guide, showing a person what was going on in their unconscious, but never dictating to them what they ought to do about it. He emphasized that he never claimed to understand a person fully – a person's inner world was their own territory and, as such, it had to be respected. Not only that – inner growth is hard work and nobody can do that work for somebody else. Jung recommended that people walk their own path steadily, one step at a time, and simply keep on doing whatever presents itself as the next thing to be done.

When people came to Jung to ask if they could be trained as analysts he always stressed that they must first work on understanding themselves. Nowadays this means that during training, analysts must undergo analysis themselves and they must continue to work on their inner world all the time. Because transference usually occurs during the course of analysis, it is very important for therapists to be well acquainted with their own neuroses and the dynamics of their own psyches – this helps them to recognize when projection is occurring. It is also a good idea for therapists to have a mentor – someone more experienced than themselves, to whom they can turn for help and advice. This is because individuation is a process that we all need to go through and is never completely finished. Unlike analysts from other schools, Jung always stressed that it is important to take feelings into account – both those of the patient and those of the analyst. He said that only if feeling is present will true healing occur – it is not possible to achieve this through working only in an analytical way 'in the head'.

One of Jung's most important pupils was Barbara Hannah (1891–1986). Born in England, she travelled to Zurich to meet Jung and stayed in Switzerland for the rest of her life, working as a psychotherapist and teaching at the CG Jung Institute. She wrote many books developing Jung's ideas.

Another major follower of Jung was Marie-Louise von Franz (1915–98), who lived in Kusnacht. She met Jung in 1933 and carried on working with him until the time of his death. She was a founder of the CG Jung Institute and wrote widely on many subjects including psychotherapy, dreams, alchemy, fairy tales and personality types.

Key aspects of Jungian analysis

Jung emphasized that every person has a unique story to tell, some aspects of which are hidden in the unconscious. It is the unfolding of this life story that provides the pathway to individuation. The key method that Jung used during the process of analysis was always one of patiently talking with and listening to people. He discovered that this was the only way really to get to know his patients and begin to unravel their unique problems. Jung laid less emphasis on childhood experiences than other psychoanalysts had done – for him the person's present life was the most important aspect. He always stressed that the spiritual aspect of human psychic experience was of vital importance and he encouraged people to realize that they are not isolated beings, but part of a great mysterious whole.

The system of psychology that Jung developed over the years provided him with a useful map of the psyche and gave structure to his therapy sessions. He used various different approaches to finding his way into a person's inner world, as discussed below.

Symbols

Jung encouraged his patients to talk about their dreams and fantasies and to explore their symbolic content. These symbolic messages provided clues as to what was going on in the person's unconscious. By discussing symbols and a person's emotional reactions towards them, Jung found that he could often bring unconscious material into conscious awareness and so begin to reach what was really bothering a person. He also saw symbols cropping up in the outer world in a synchronous way.

Archetypal messages

Many symbolic messages that emerge from the unconscious turn out to be archetypal in nature. Jung often worked with these symbols in a constructive way, using a process of **amplification**. This meant that he would discuss possible connections with symbolism in myth, folklore and religion, in order to arrive at clarification and enhanced meaning. He was exploring the collective content of dreams and fantasies, rather than just interpreting them from an individual viewpoint.

Association

Given an original image or idea, Jung would encourage the patient to follow a train of spontaneous connected thoughts. He believed that these were always meaningful in one way or another, and might uncover unconscious complexes.

Active imagination

Jung believed that the flow of images that take place in the form of dreams while we are asleep also carry on during our waking hours as undercurrents of fantasy. He said that these fantasies were real psychic entities and that it was very important to stay in touch with the unconscious by exploring them. To do this you enter a day-dreaming state, halfway between sleep and waking, and observe the images and fantasies that arise. This allows the psyche freedom and space to express itself. Jung emphasized that it was also important to enter into the process fully and interact with the fantasy images: otherwise the fantasies merely flow by you and you remain unaffected by them. He encouraged people to explore the symbolism emerging from the unconscious in creative ways such as drawing, painting, drama, writing or modelling in clay. The whole active imagination process is like play – bringing the person back to a child-like state that allows the unconscious to express itself more freely.

Barbara Hannah gave Jung credit for rediscovering active imagination rather than inventing it, pointing out that people had used similar processes since the dawn of time. Jung developed the process when he decided that simply analysing dreams was not enough – he wanted to take the process a stage further, and work actively with the symbolism that emerged. Jung never interfered with the active imagination process because he believed that it should be allowed to develop spontaneously and he did not want to influence it in any way. He simply encouraged people to work in this way and tell him about what they had done: this approach helped people to take charge of their own life and individuation process. Jung used active imagination hand in hand with dream analysis.

Creative visualization

The fact that Jung also intuitively used another technique which is closely related to active imagination, is shown in an anecdote included in Aniela Jaffe's book *Jung's Last Years*. Nowadays this technique is sometimes known as 'creative visualization'. Unlike active imagination, during creative visualization it is the therapist who is in charge of the process. While the client is in a relaxed state similar to light hypnosis, the therapist usually takes the client on an inner journey, perhaps describing a vivid scene which may help the person to relax. On the occasion described by Aniela Jaffe, Jung was talking to a young schoolteacher who had been suffering from almost total insomnia. He only had one session in which to help her and time was short as he tried to describe to her how he himself found relaxation by sailing on the lake and letting himself drift with the wind. He could tell by her eyes that she didn't really understand, but then, as he went on describing the peaceful scene to her, he began to sing a Rhine lullaby that his mother had used when he was a child. As he sang he could see that she had become fully relaxed and was in a light trance. Two years later he encountered the doctor who had referred the woman to him, and the man pressed him to explain what kind of therapy he had used, because after the consultation her insomnia had vanished, never to return. Jung, being so far ahead of his time in using such an unorthodox method, was somewhat put on the spot and at a loss to explain.

Balancing of opposites

Jung frequently emphasized the process of balancing of opposites, which is necessary to achieve a healthy, integrated psyche. Once two conflicting opposite trends are brought into consciousness the tension between them can be resolved. A third state, representing a new, more healthy attitude can now emerge. Jung called this third state the **transcendent function**.

Treating the psyche as a reality

Jung always emphasized that for him the contents of the psyche had concrete reality. He sometimes used methods not unlike those used by shamans, where a person is encouraged to visualize aspects of their inner world in this way. One of his patients, Jane Wheelwright, describes how she confessed to him that she felt she was going mad – a common fear when one is close to uncovering collective contents of the unconscious. Jung made a grab in the air towards her, as if he was catching a football, and then hugged it to his chest, telling her that now he had it and she need fear no longer. This evidently worked, because from then on her fear disappeared.

Criticisms of Jung

Like all great thinkers, Jung has had plenty of critics. Some of them have accused him of being domineering and egotistical, determined to collect devoted admirers in the academic world. Others have suggested he had a selfish side, saying that he lived off his wife's fortune and was a womanizer – sour grapes perhaps! Many dismissed him as an unscientific, mystical thinker, immersed in a fantasy world. Still others have accused him of anti-Semitism, and debate still occasionally crops up about the nature of his involvement with the Nazis.

This accusation first arose in the early 1930s, when Jung accepted the vacant presidency of the General Medical Society for Psychotherapy, and took over as editor of its magazine the *Zentralblatt*. Both were located in Germany, just at the time Hitler came into power, and people were being forced to conform to Nazi ideas. As a Swiss citizen, Jung was well aware of the dangers of the ideology of the Society becoming too one-sided. He set to work altering the balance of membership, which had previously been predominantly German, and the Society evolved into the International General Society for

Psychotherapy. He saw this new balance as being important not only to allay people's fears, but also to protect the German people from what he saw as an increasing spiritual isolation.

Unfortunately, the first issue of the *Zentralblatt* that saw Jung as editor sparked off a damaging controversy. Without his knowledge, and against his orders, it contained a special supplement that was supposed to be included only in the German edition. This supplement was aimed at German society members, obliging them to adopt Hitler's ideology. Not only that, but the same edition also carried an editorial by Jung, outlining differences between German and Jewish psychology. This was intended simply as a study in comparative psychology, much like comparing say the English and the Americans. But it was incredibly bad timing in such a period of racial unrest and quite naturally it unleashed a torrent of criticism.

Jung found himself having to make an agonizing decision – should he stay in the Society and give backing to his friends in the scientific community, at the same time risking further accusations of anti-Semitism and Nazi collaboration? In point of fact, many of his friends in the Society were actually Jews. Later, various documents came to light that showed that Jung had played a major part in advising Jewish friends and helping them to escape to England and America. He also supported the rights of Jewish members of the Society who attempted to speak out against Nazi pressure. Eventually Jung resigned from the Society in 1939, because he totally disagreed with those who encouraged discrimination along non-Aryan lines. By this stage he was becomingly increasingly and openly hostile to the Nazi regime. His books were banned in Germany and destroyed elsewhere in Europe; at one point, now that he was on the Nazi blacklist, he had to flee from his home in Zurich to safety in the mountains. Accusations of Nazi collaboration still occasionally get levelled at Jung, but one has only to read what he has to say in his books to see that this has more to do with lucrative and sensational journalism than with the truth. Jung was interested in healing people and encouraging them to grow as individuals rather than in dark power and dictatorship.

Jung was always very popular with women and his discovery of his own anima meant that he was a pioneer figure in promoting the idea that we all have a masculine and a feminine aspect. Theoretically he supported women and wanted them to have equal rights and make their own way in the world. Nevertheless he was a man of his times in many ways and his attitude was sometimes rather patriarchal and paternalistic. Jane Wheeler found it very irritating, for example, when she tried to make an appointment with him and he said that he would discuss the time and date with her husband! She felt that this reflected in him an attitude that saw men as the controllers of the fate of women. This attitude is slow to change and many women in the world are still struggling with it even today. Jane Wheeler added that it was through working with Jung that she was able to outgrow total dependence on his ideas and develop some of her own. Helping people to maturity in this way was the main point of Jung's work.

Jung's psychology has sometimes been attacked for encouraging people to concentrate mostly upon the self – critics say that he does not give enough attention to relationships with others. However, Jung argues that we cannot hope to relate well to others until we can see ourselves clearly. He says that in fact it is not possible to separate the relationship with the Self from the relationship with others. 'Relationship to the Self is at once relationship to our fellow man, and no one can be related to the latter until he is related to himself.'

Into the future

For Jung, life was a sacred journey with meaning and purpose. His interests were very wide-ranging and he wrote extensively upon many different subjects. But above all he was a psychologist and analyst and it is this aspect of his work that most people come to first. His **analytical method** gradually strips away built-up defensive layers of the personality until we are able to see our true selves. The goal is to achieve a wider, fuller consciousness, less dependent upon ego. This new consciousness is no longer totally egocentric, obsessed with its own petty needs and endlessly using unconscious ploys to cover up its inadequacies.

Jung's influence has also extended far beyond his private work as a psychologist, making him one of the greatest thinkers of the twentieth century:

- His ideas about the collective unconscious and archetypes have given us new insights into the structure and evolution of the human psyche.
- His lifelong interest in dreams has expanded our understanding of the mysterious world of the unconscious.

- Many of his ideas about personality, such as introversion and extroversion have become part of everyday language and understanding.
- His fascination with mythology, religion and the paranormal has encouraged people to open up new thinking about spiritual psychology.
- Jungian analysts are now trained all over the world and there are many institutions devoted to expanding and building upon his ideas.

Jung's charismatic personality has inspired many people and taught us to look deeply within ourselves and begin to accept ourselves for who we truly are. Ultimately, this is a spiritual journey, one that Jung himself saw as being essential if mankind were to have a future. It is this conscious awareness and fulfilment of one's own unique being – the individuation process – that is the pathway and the goal of Jungian analysis.

Jung always emphasized the importance of the individual viewpoint. He said that he did not want anybody to be a 'Jungian', but rather to find their own truth and be themselves. In a letter to Freud he said, 'should I be found one day only to have created another "ism" then I will have failed in all I tried to do.'

Jung was truly himself right up to the end, when he died peacefully at home on 6 June 1961, surrounded by his family. Shortly before his death two small strokes left him bedridden, and during this time he had prophetic visions in which he saw enormous stretches of the earth laid waste, but thankfully not the whole planet. Three days before he died he sent his son Franz to the cellar, uttering the now famous words, 'let's have a really good wine tonight.'

Synchronous events surrounded Jung right up until his death. The day he died his friend, writer and visionary Laurens van der Post, who was voyaging from Africa to Europe at the time, had a dream of Jung waving goodbye. The same day Barbara Hannah discovered that her car battery had suddenly run down completely. And his death was appropriately followed a few hours later by a violent storm, during which lightning struck his favourite poplar tree by the lake. In the last days he had seemed peaceful and serene: he remarked that he knew there was only one small piece remaining to complete his knowledge of the truth. In what was probably his last 'big' dream, he saw a huge round stone on a high plateau. At its foot were engraved the words 'And this shall be a sign unto you of Wholeness and Oneness.' His journey through life was complete.

Summary

- Jung travelled extensively and made comparative studies of culture and religion in order to increase his understanding of human psychology.
- He believed that in order to heal, people need to learn to listen to messages from their unconscious minds.
- He always encouraged people to follow their own path and think independently.
- In order to access messages from the unconscious Jung used interactive and creative methods of therapy, including dreamwork and active imagination.
- He said that it was always important to take feelings into account as well as simply analysing the psyche and its contents.
- Jung emphasized that in order to become an analyst one must first try to understand oneself.

Alchemy An esoteric practice combining aspects of mysticism, magic, science and religion.

Amplification Exploring symbolic meanings by comparisons with myth, folklore and religion.

Analytical method Method of studying things by breaking them down into their separate elements.

Anima The unconscious feminine side of a man's personality.

Animus The unconscious masculine side of a woman's personality.

Archetype A universally recognizable image, or pattern of thinking, which represents a typical human experience.

Causality The idea that related events are connected by cause and effect.

Collective unconscious The deepest layer of the unconscious, which extends beyond the individual psyche.

Complex A related group of emotionally charged unconscious ideas, thoughts and images.

Cryptomnesia An experience that is forgotten before later being reproduced without the person recognizing it as a memory.

Divination Insight into the future or the unknown, gained by paranormal methods.

Ego The centre of consciousness and the sense of identity.

Esoteric To do with inner knowledge; from the Greek *esoterikos*, meaning 'within'. Sometimes used to refer to secret or mystical knowledge revealed only to a chosen few.

Extroversion Direction of interest outwards towards external objects and relationships.

Gnostic Relating to knowledge, especially occult mystical knowledge.

Halcyon Means calm, peaceful and happy, and the word also refers to kingfishers.

Individuation Conscious realization and fulfilment of the Self.

Introversion Direction of interest inwards towards the inner world of thoughts and feelings.

Intuitive Knowing things without having to reason them out.

Libido Motivating psychic energy.

Mandala A symbolic circular figure that represents the universe, or the wholeness of the Self.

Mechanistic A view that sees a person as a machine whose behaviour is determined by physical or chemical causes.

Mythopoeic To do with the making of myths.

Myths Traditional stories that try to explain natural, social or religious ideas.

Neurosis A minor nervous or mental disorder.

Numinous Awe-inspiring; indicating the presence of the divine.

Occult Secret knowledge concerning the mysterious, paranormal or magical.

Paranormal Things that cannot be explained by normal, objective methods.

Parapsychology The study of paranormal mental phenomena.

Persona The public face that a person assumes when relating to others.

Positivism A way of thinking that limits knowledge to that which is directly observable.

Precognition Knowing something in advance, often by paranormal means.

Projection A process whereby an unconscious characteristic, a fault, or even a talent of one's own is seen as belonging to another person or object.

Psyche The mind, soul or spirit.

Psychiatrist Someone who studies and treats mental and nervous disorders.

Psychoanalysis A system of psychology and method of treating mental disorders, originally developed by Sigmund Freud.

Psychogenic disorders Disorders that originate with mental conditions – physical symptoms may follow on.

Psychologist Scientist who studies the mind and behaviour.

Psychosis Severe mental disorder.

Reductionism A way of thinking that breaks complex ideas down into simple component parts.

Repression A process of banishing unpleasant or undesirable feelings and experiences to the unconscious mind.

Self The archetype of wholeness of the psyche that transcends the ego.

Shadow The unconscious part of the personality that contains characteristics which one cannot recognize as one's own.

Spiritual Concerned with the spirit, i.e. the intelligent non-physical part of a person, as opposed to the physical body.

Synchronicity The simultaneous occurrence of two meaningful but not causally connected events.

Transcendent function A new, more healthy attitude that emerges in the psyche when two opposite functions become integrated.

Transference Emotional involvement between patient and therapist.

Unconscious Parts of the mind and personality that a person is not aware of.

Zeitgeist The spirit of the age.

taking it further

In this section you will find:
- a timeline of important events in Jung's life
- places to visit
- a list of Jung's most important works
- a further reading list
- useful websites.

Timeline of important events in Jung's life

1875	Born on 26 July, in Kesswil, Switzerland
1879	Family moves to Basel
1884	Birth of sister Gertrude
1895–1900	Studies medicine at University of Basel
1896	Death of father
1900	Works as assistant physician under Eugen Bleuler at Burghölzli
1902	Awarded Ph.D. from university of Zürich; studies briefly under French psychologist Pierre Janet in Paris; visits London
1903	Marries Emma Rauschenbach
1904	Birth of daughter Agathe
1903-5	Works on research in word association
1905	Becomes lecturer in psychiatry at the University of Zürich;
1906	Birth of daughter Gret
1905–09	Senior staff physician at Burghölzli Psychiatric Clinic; correspondence with Freud begins
1907	Meets Freud; writes *The Psychology of Dementia Praecox*
1908	First International Psychoanalytic Congress, Salzburg; birth of son Franz
1909	Gives up working at Burghölzli and moves to Küsnacht, Zurich, to start private practice; goes to America with Freud on lecture tour and receives honorary degree from Clark University

1910	Writes *Symbols of Transformation*; birth of daughter Marianne
1910–13	President of the International Psychoanalytic Association
1912	Publishes *Psychology of the Unconscious*
1913	Final split with Freud; resigns lectureship at Zurich University
1913–19	Midlife crisis – confronts unconscious
1914	Resigns as president of the International Psychoanalytic Association; birth of daughter Helene
1918	Commandant of camp for British interns at Chateau d'Oex
1920	Visits Algiers and Tunis
1921	Publishes *Psychological Types*
1922	Purchase of land at Bollingen
1923	Begins building his tower at Bollingen; death of mother
1924	Studies Pueblo Indians in New Mexico
1926	Studies inhabitants of Mount Elgon, Kenya
1928	Begins to study alchemy
1932	Awarded literature prize of the City of Zurich
1933	Awarded professorship of Psychology at the Federal Polytechnical University of Zurich; edits the Central Journal for Psychotherapy and Related Fields until 1939; publishes *Modern Man in Search of a Soul*
1935	Made president of the Swiss Society for Practical Psychology; publishes *Analytical Psychology: its Theory and Practice*; delivers Tavistock lectures in London

1936	Honorary doctorate from Harvard
1938	Visits India; honorary doctorate from Calcutta, Benares, Allahabad; President of International Congress for Psychotherapy at Oxford – receives honorary doctorate from Oxford University
1941	Retires from the Federal Polytechnical University of Zurich
1943	Made Professor of Medical Psychology at the University of Basel; also made honorary member of the Swiss Academy of Sciences
1944	Resigns chair at Basel because of a critical illness; publishes *Psychology and Alchemy*
1945	Honorary doctorate from Geneva University on his 70th birthday
1948	Founding of CG Jung institute, Zurich
1951	Publishes *Aion*
1952	Publishes *Answer to Job*
1955	Death of his wife Emma
1956	Publishes *Mysterium Coniunctionis*
1957	Starts work on *Memories, Dreams, Reflections*; publishes *The Undiscovered Self*; BBC TV interview
1960	Made honorary citizen of Küsnacht on his 85th birthday
1961	Finishes *Man and His Symbols,* ten days before his death; dies in Kusnacht 6 June

Places to visit

Kesswil

Jung's birthplace on the shore of Lake Constance in NE Switzerland. It is a small and pretty fishing village with half-timbered houses. A street is named after Jung and there is a commemorative plaque on the presbytery where he was born, describing him as 'explorer of the human soul and its hidden depths'. You can also visit the small church where his father was parson, with its lovingly kept cemetery full of flowers.

Küsnacht

The CG Jung Institute, Hornweg 28, CH-8700,

Founded in 1948 as a centre for training in and researching analytical psychology and psychotherapy. The institute is now an international meeting place for the exchange of ideas, and holds many events and lectures. It has a large library of material relating to Jung and his work, and you can also buy and order books.

Jung is buried at Küsnacht, in a family grave at the protestant church, along with his parents, wife and sister. There is a large gravestone, decorated with the epitaph:

'The first man comes from the earth and is of the earth. Invoked or not invoked, the god is present. The second man comes from heaven and is of heaven.'

Bollingen

Jung built a tower here, starting in 1923. It is about 40 km from Zurich, on the shore of the lake. It was a peaceful place where he could escape from everyday life and find the space to think and be himself. There is a stone monument which he erected in 1950, explaining what the tower meant to him.

A list of Jung's most important works

Jung was a prolific writer and wrote many essays, papers, lectures and letters as well as full-length books. By his own admission his work became vast and chaotic, but fortunately there is a complete collection, *The Collected Works of CG Jung* (see **Further reading**). Here is a list of some of his important works, in chronological order.

1902 MD dissertation, *On the Psychology and Pathology of So-called Occult Phenomena*

1903 *Studies in Word-Association*

1907 *The Psychology of Dementia Praecox*

1910 *Symbols of Transformation*

1912 *Psychology of the Unconscious*

1916 *Seven Sermons to the Dead*
      Collected Papers on Analytical Psychology

1918 *The Role of the Unconscious*
      Instinct and the Unconscious

1921 *Psychological Types*

1921 *The Secret of the Golden Flower* (with Richard Wilhelm)
      Contributions to Analytical Psychology

1933 *Modern Man in Search of a Soul*

1935 *Analytical Psychology – Its Theory and Practice*

1944 *Psychology and Alchemy*

1951 *Aion*

1952 *Answer to Job*

1956 *Mysterium Coniunctionis*

1957 *The Undiscovered Self*

1958 *Flying Saucers – a Modern Myth*

1963 *Memories, Dreams, Reflections* (published posthumously)

1964 *Man and His Symbols* (also published posthumously)

Further reading

There are huge numbers of books available both by and about Jung. The following brief list offers a few suggestions for where to begin further reading.

Books written by Jung

The Collected Works of CG Jung, UK edition: Routledge and Kegan Paul, 1953–71; US edition: Bollinger Foundation, Princeton University Press, 1967.

The 20 volumes cover the following subjects:

1 *Psychiatric Studies*
2 *Experimental Researches*
3 *The Psychogenesis of Mental Disease*
4 *Freud and Psychoanalysis*
5 *Symbols of Transformation*
6 *Psychological Types*
7 *Two Essays on Analytical Psychology*
8 *The Structure and Dynamics of the Psyche*
9 *The Archetypes and the Collective Unconscious; Aion*
10 *Civilization in Transition*
11 *Psychology and Religion: West and East*
12 *Psychology and Alchemy*
13 *Alchemical Studies*
14 *Mysterium Coniunctionis*
15 *The Spirit in Man, Art and Literature*
16 *The Practice of Psychotherapy*
17 *The Development of Personality*
18 *The Symbolic Life*
19 *General Bibliography of Jung's Writings*
20 *General Index to the Collected Works*

Separate books by Jung include the following:

Memories, Dreams, Reflections, Routledge and Kegan Paul, 1963 and Collins/Fontana, 1967. This is Jung's autobiography, recorded and edited by his secretary, Aniela Jaffe. It is one of the best introductions to Jung.

Modern Man in Search of a Soul, Routledge, 1933

Man and His Symbols, Aldus Books, 1964 and Picador, 1978

Analytical Psychology: its Theory and Practice (The Tavistock Lectures), Routledge and Kegan Paul, 1968

Answer to Job, Routledge, 1954

The Freud/Jung Letters, edited by William McGuire, The Hogarth Press and Routledge and Kegan Paul, 1974

A useful map to guide you around Jung's extensive works is:

Hopcke, R. H. (1989) *A Guided Tour of the Collected works of C G Jung,* Shambala

Books about Jung

McLynn, F. (1996) *Carl Gustav Jung,* Bantam Press

Fordham, F. (1991) *An Introduction to Jung's Psychology,* Penguin

Stevens, A. (1991) *On Jung,* Penguin

van der Post, L. (1975) *Jung and the Story of Our Time,* Random House

Jaffé, A. (1984) *Jung's Last Years,* Spring Publications Inc.

Wehr, G. (1987) *Jung: A Biography,* Shambhala

Hannah, B. (1991) *Jung: His Life and Work,* Shambhala

Dunne, C. (2000) *Carl Jung: Wounded Healer of the Soul,* Continuum

Developing Jung's ideas further

Neumann, E. (1970) *The Origins and History of Consciousness,* Princeton University Press

Jung, E. (1983) *Animus and Anima,* Spring Publications

Hannah, B. (1985) *Encounters with the Soul: Imagination as Developed by C G Jung,* Sigo Press (Chiron, 2001).

Useful websites

www.psy.pdx.edu Psychology resource site with lots of links

www.psywww.com Very useful site with psychology-related information

www.answers.com Handy site with a lot of links

www.jungian-analysis.org Site of the Society of Jungian Analysis

www.cgjungclinic.org.uk Clinic related to the Society of Jungian Analysis

www.jungnewyork.com Information about Jungian analysis

www.cgjungpage.org Comprehensive site offering articles, discussion forums and a directory of analysts

www.dcdata.com/jung Abstracts of Jung's *Collected Works*

There are many other websites that offer information about Jung and analytical psychology. You can also find some of his letters online, including correspondence with Sigmund Freud.

index